FROM THE HUB

TO THE HUDSON:

WITH SKETCHES OF

Nature, History and Industry

IN

NORTH-WESTERN MASSACHUSETTS.

BY

WASHINGTON GLADDEN.

BOSTON:
THE NEW ENGLAND NEWS COMPANY.
1869.

Samuel Bowles & Company,
Electrotypers, Printers and Binders,
Springfield, Mass.

PREFACE.

In the collection of materials for this little book I have been assisted by many friends; among whom are Messrs. Stevens of the Mansion House in Greenfield; and Rev. Robert Crawford, D. D., Nathaniel Hitchcock, Esq., and Dr. Charles Williams of Deerfield. Hitchcock's Geological Report, Holland's History of Western Massachusetts, Hoyt's Indian Wars, Barber's Historical Collections, and the various reports of Commissioners and Engineers upon the Hoosac Tunnel, have been of great service to me. The engravings of the Tunnel were executed from photographs by Messrs. Hurd & Ward of North Adams.

The book is built on these two maxims:

1. History begins at home.

2. It is better to see one town from all its hill-tops than five hundred towns from the car windows.

The reader will find upon its pages extended

notices of various persons and industries. I ask him to take my word for it that these are not purchased puffs, and they were not prompted by that species of gratitude peculiar to politicians—"a lively sense of favors yet to come."

My first purpose was to let the book be anonymous, from a foolish feeling that such work might be considered unprofessional; but I have concluded that the attempt to show people how and where they may cheaply and pleasantly spend their few days of summer vacation—often the dreariest days of the year—is nothing to be ashamed of or apologized for. A book that helps anybody to see and enjoy the Connecticut Valley or the Berkshire Hills, will be likely to do less harm than a book about the Mode of Baptism or the Origin of Evil. I do not, however, pretend to have been wholly actuated by considerations of benevolence. I have enjoyed the writing of the book. It may be death to my readers, but it has been sport for me.

The rest of the preface will be found in the body of the book. W. G.

NORTH ADAMS, May 1, 1869.

From the Hub to the Hudson.

CHAPTER I.

FROM BOSTON TO GREENFIELD.

A CERTAIN Vermont Yankee, extolling, as Yankees are wont to do, the town of his nativity, mentioned as one of its distinguishing peculiarities the remarkable fact that you could start from there to go to any place in creation. The Yankee who hails from Boston may, without exceeding his usual modesty, make the same claim for the place of his residence. Boston is a good place to start from. Indeed it is said that pretty much everything that moves in this world has started, or does start, from Boston. Here the fires of revolutionary patriotism were kindled; here is Faneuil Hall, and the Old South Church; here John Hancock learned to write that large hand which so boldly leads the column of signatures to the famous declaration; here Adams spoke, and Otis wrote, and Warren fought and fell. Out of Boston came the Radical Abolitionists; forth from Boston proceed the apostoli and the apostolae of the new gospel of Woman Suffrage; and from the pent-up confines of this crooked town issue those twin prodigies of literature and statesmanship, George Francis Train and the Count Johannes. Who can deny that Boston is the proper base of all operations, and the perspective point from which the world must be pictured and regarded?

It was inevitable, then, that our book should begin at Boston. And as charity which begins at home is often greatly minded to stay there, so the book which begins at Boston is not likely to get far beyond it. Being at the center of the universe, the centripetal force is almost irresistible. But the centrifugal impulses are sometimes felt, even in Boston, as everybody knows, and taking advantage of the first wave of outward movement, we will fly from the hub toward the periphery.

Very likely, however, there will be numerous travelers seeking the shadows of the Berkshire hills and the quiet of the Connecticut meadows, for whom Boston will not be the natural starting-point. It is not given to all of us to breathe the atmosphere of this classic town, nor to be blown upon by its east winds, nor to sneeze with its influenza. And such as have been denied these happy distinguishments of fortune may not care to read any further in this chapter. From them we will part company here, in the hope of meeting them a little nearer to sunset.

One word before we go any further. This is not a

guide-book. If you bought it for that, you are badly cheated. The guide-book knows everything; and there are a great many things that this little book does not know. The guide-book stops at all the towns; this book will trundle right through many of them, not even halting five minutes for refreshments. The guide-book knows just how many meeting-houses, court-houses, school-houses, banks, jails, mills, stores, each town contains; how long all the rivers are; how deep the lakes; how high the mountains. This little book confesses its ignorance of many of these things. It does not mean to burden its readers with many statistics; it seeks to be a pleasant companion not only to railway travelers, but also to fireside travelers. And if, without attempting any exhaustive account of the region where its scenes are laid, it shall succeed in calling attention to some of its most attractive features, and in bringing back some of the associations of the olden time, the end for which it was written will be attained.

All this might have been said in the preface, but people never read prefaces.

Having a good start and a fair understanding, we roll out of the noble granite passenger-house of the Fitchburg Railway, and are soon crossing the Charles River upon one of the many viaducts and bridges which span that stream. To the right is Charlestown, with Breed's Hill and Bunker's Hill; the former of which is crowned by the famous obelisk that marks the spot where Prescott and Putnam and their brave provincials planted the tree of liberty; the latter of which is surmounted by a costly Roman Catholic cathedral. Bunker Hill monument divides the honors now with half a dozen brick smoke-stacks; some of which appear from this point even taller than the monumental shaft. So, too often, are the great events of history overtopped or obscured by the nearer but meaner facts of daily use and custom.

On the left, the old bridge crosses from Boston to Cambridgeport; and on the top of Beacon Hill the dome of the State House remains the most conspicuous figure of the landscape, well guarded by the sentinel spires of Park Street and Somerset Street churches.

East Cambridge welcomes us to its hospitable, but not very attractive shores; and the view we get of old Cambridge, further on, is not one that does justice to its beauty. Is it Holmes, or was it Hawthorne, who once told us that the railroads almost always take us past the back doors and show us the worst sides of houses and towns? The rule has some exceptions, but old Cambridge is not one of them. There is an excellent flavor of age and respectability about this ancient town, if you know how to take it. "Doubtless God could have made a better, but doubtless he never did," quoth our worthy Hosea Biglow. We shall be compelled to take his word for it, while we whistle through the outskirts of what might, but for a few ancient elms along the railway, pass for a first-class western "city."

Belmont next puts in an excellent appearance. It is one of the neatest of the "subhubs;" its charming residences on either side the railway must prove a delightful resort to men whose days are spent in the narrow and noisy streets of Boston.

Waverly is a pleasant name for a pleasant place. Like the capital of the country, it is a village of magnificent distances; like the other Waverly, it is largely a work of fiction, though founded on fact.

Waltham—here we come to the solid realities again. This is the western end of old Watertown, and was separately incorporated in 1738. The occasion of the division of the town was a church quarrel. The old church edifice was at the eastern end of the town, and the inhabitants of that section were determined to keep it there; but the star of empire led the tides of population westward; and since the dwellers in the ancient burg would not be content with the church that was built midway, they were obliged to have the town divided, and the Walthamites sat down under their own vine and fig-tree, by the banks of the smooth flowing Charles. Waltham is a very substantial and thrifty town of something less than ten thousand inhabitants. Eight churches offer to worshipers all varieties of faith and form; a public library of 4,500 volumes carries on the education begun in the excellent schools; a Savings' Bank holds the accumulations of the mechanics and operatives who constitute the population; and two weekly newspapers, one radical and the other neutral, furnish those of the people who are not able to think for themselves with ready made opinions on all sorts of subjects.

The large brick factory on your left, nearly opposite the railway station, is the cotton mill of the Boston Manufacturing Company. Here was erected, in 1814, the first power-loom for cotton weaving ever operated in America. In this large establishment, (then much smaller than now,) the great cotton manufacturing interest in America had its origin. A little pamphlet, by Hon. Nathan Appleton of Boston, giving the history of the beginning and the growth of this enterprise, is as interesting as a romance, not only to all who make cotton goods but to all who wear them. The project was formed by Mr. Francis C. Lowell, while in Edinburgh, in the year 1811. At that place he and Mr. Appleton discussed the practicability of weaving cotton cloth by power; and before he returned to this country Mr. Lowell visited Manchester to gain all possible information upon the subject. As the result of these deliberations, the Boston Manufacturing Company was formed in 1813, this water-privilege at Waltham was purchased, and the machinery was procured.

"The power-loom was at this time being introduced in England; but its construction was kept very secret, and, after many failures, public opinion was not favorable to its success. Mr. Lowell had obtained all the information which was practicable about it, and was determined to perfect it himself. He was for some months experimenting at a store in Broad Street, employing a man to turn a crank. It was not until the new building at Waltham was completed, and other machinery was running, that the first loom was ready for trial. Many little matters were to be overcome or adjusted before it would work perfectly. Mr. Lowell said to me that he did not wish me to see it until it was complete, of which he would give me notice. At length the time arrived. He invited me to go out with him and see the loom operate. I well remember the state of admiration and satisfaction with which we sat by the loom; watching the beautiful movement of this new and wonderful machine, destined, as it evidently was, to change the character of all textile industry. This was in the autumn of 1814.

"Mr. Lowell's loom was different in several particulars from the English loom, which was afterwards made public. The principal movement was by a cam, revolving with an eccentric motion, which has since given place to the crank motion now universally used. Some other minor improvements have since been introduced, mostly tending to give it increased speed.

"The article first made at Waltham was precisely the article of which a large portion of the manufacture of the country has continued to consist—a heavy sheeting of No. 14 yarn, 37 inches wide, 44 picks to the inch, and weighing something less than three yards to the pound."*

These goods were sold in 1816 for 30 cents per yard; in 1819, for 21 cents; in 1826, for 13 cents; in 1829, for 8 1-2 cents; in 1843, for 6 1-2 cents,—the lowest figure they ever reached. They are now (March,

* *Introduction of the Power Loom:* By Nathan Appleton.

1869,) quoted in the New York wholesale markets at about 13 cents a yard.

The property of this company now consists of two mills for making cloth, containing 40,000 spindles and 700 looms; one mill for making hosiery, turning out about 600 dozen per day; and a bleachery and dye works, with facilities for bleaching and dyeing about six millions of pounds of cotton cloth per annum. It employs about 1,300 hands, and has a capital stock of $600,000.

Another famous industrial establishment is found at Waltham. As we leave the village going westward, the shops of the Waltham Watch Company down by the banks of the river attract our notice. The main building is more than 300 feet long, with wings and cross-wings more than doubling this space. Three-quarters of a mile of benches are surrounded by 750 operators, about one-third of whom are women and girls of American parentage. If you should walk up the main street in time to meet these work people going to dinner, you would be pleasantly impressed by their intelligent countenances, their neat attire, and their orderly manners. You might travel far before meeting in one company no larger than this an equal number of thoughtful and cultivated faces. Since about 350,000 of the watches made by this company have found their way into the pockets of the American people, it is safe to suppose that its history and its methods of operation are not altogether unknown. Unlike the Swiss and other foreign watches, every part of the Waltham watch is made by some delicate and ingenious machine. No such large manufactories of watches are found in the Old World. In Geneva, since all the work is done by hand, the operatives take it to their homes, and each one spends his life-time in making one particular piece of the mechanism. Machine work being more uniform and accurate than hand work, the Waltham watches ought to keep better time than foreign watches, and this we believe is the verdict of experience.

This view on our left as we leave the village of Waltham is a very charming one,—the Charles River at our feet in the foreground, and winding gracefully through the valley; the village of Waltham, scattered over an undulating plain, and the low hills in the distance toward Newton.

Stony Brook is the name of the next station. The brook which gives the station its name is in the foreground on the right, and is not remarkably stony either.

Weston comes next, and a single fact in its history must suffice us. After having been twice directed to procure a preacher, this town was at length, in 1706, prosecuted at the Court of Sessions for not having a settled minister. The instances are not frequent in our day, let us trust, in which people are compelled to resort to the law in order to obtain the gospel.

Lincoln is only a crossing and a depot; leaving which, we are soon plunging into the Walden woods, and skirting along the Walden pond, made immortal by the hermit of Concord. It is a beautiful region.

The quiet woods and the placid lake might tempt to hermithood one less fond of nature than Thoreau. On the western shore of the lake, however, we discover evidences that this solitude would not be so welcome to the gentle philosopher if he should return to it. Here are huts, and swings, and platforms, designed to accommodate picnics; and it is more than likely if the day is pleasant that the woods are filled with a frolicing company of Sunday-school children, or a crowd of Teutons guzzling lager, and singing about "der Doitcher Fodderlant." Just beyond the woods, a wide view opens on the left across level meadows, and in the western horizon Mount Wachusett, nearly thirty miles distant, in the town of Princeton, is plainly seen on a clear day.

The next shriek of the locomotive means discord if it means anything; but the conductor looking in just now, says "*Concord;*" and it is impossible to doubt him. "In 1635," says the chronicler, "Musketaquid was purchased from the Indians and called Concord, on account of the peaceable manner in which it was obtained." Strange that the town which was so amicably settled should have been the town where the first battle of the revolution was fought! In Johnson's "*Wonder Working Providence*," a quaint old Puritan record, we find some account of the early settlers. After describing the miserable huts in which they first found shelter, he goes on to say:

"Yet in these poor wigwams they sing psalmes, pray and praise their God till they can provide them houses, which ordinarily was not wont to be with many till the earth by the Lord's blessing brought forth bread to feed them, their wives and their little ones, which with sore labours they attain ; every one that can lift a hoe to strike it into the earth standing stoutly to their labours, and tear up the rootes and bushes which the first yeare bears them a very thin crop, till the soard of the earth be rotten, and therefore they have been forced *to cut their bread very thin* for a long season. But the Lord is pleased to provide for them great store of fish in the spring time, and especially Alewives about the bignesse of a Herring. Many thousands of these they used to put under their Indian corn which they plant in hills five foote asunder. . . . . The want of English graine, wheate, barley and rice proved a sore affliction to some stomacks who could not live upon Indian bread and water, yet were they compelled to it till cattell increased and the plowes could but goe. Instead of apples and pears they had pomkins and squashes of divers kinds. . . . . Thus this poore people populate this howling desert, marching manfully on (the Lord asisting) through the greatest difficulties and sorest labors that ever any with such weak means have done."

Under such schooling as this the men of Concord learned the steadfastness and heroism that they needed in after days. The stuff that was bred in them by these hardships was inherited by their descendants ; and at length, one bright morning, a hundred and forty years after this battle with hunger and cold was begun, the echoes of a more illustrious if not a fiercer conflict were heard among the Concord Hills.

It would be worth our while, could we spare a few hours in our journey, to stop at this ancient town, and take a stroll through its quiet streets, and its memorable places. We should find it a remarkably well-preserved old village; not a squalid building is to be seen; many of the houses bear marks of age, but all are neat and many are tasteful and elegant. The principal street is one of the pleasantest in New England. There is not much noise of business, but an air of thrift and cultivation pervades the place. Here have dwelt and are dwelling now a larger number of famous people than one small village commonly contains. Here our great Hawthorne lived and died. Here Marcus Antoninus reappears with the physiognomy of a true Yankee, bearing the title of the "Sage of Concord," and answering to the name of Ralph Waldo Emerson; here Alcott the seer, and his daughter Louisa, whose vision is not much duller than her father's, spend their days; here the brilliant Thoreau found a residence, and here those who loved and cared for him to the last are living yet; here is the home of Mrs. Jane G. Austin, one whom the novel-reading world knows well; here Frederick Hudson, for many years the wheel-horse of the New York *Herald*, is trying to repair the frame he has broken with too much toil; here dwells Judge Hoar, the jurist, the scholar, the orator, the wit, and the noblest Roman of them all. Time would fail us if we tried to note the stars of lesser magnitude in the Concord constellation.

Any one will show you the road that leads to the spot where on the 19th of April, 1775, the Revolutionary War began. The day before, at Lexington, the American militia had been fired on by Pitcairn's British regulars, and eight of them had been killed; but no shot was fired in return. Here, where the North Bridge formerly crossed the Concord River, the first battle was fought. The bridge is now removed, and the highway which led to it is enclosed; but a monument marks the spot where the British soldiers were posted when the engagement began, and directly across the river in what is now a quiet meadow, the place is seen where

> "the embattled farmers stood
> And fired the shot heard round the world."

The British, as everybody knows, had gained possession of the town, and were destroying the stores gathered by the provincials in anticipation of war; while the militiamen had assembled outside the village, and across the stream, partly because unwilling to begin hostilities, partly because greatly inferior in numbers to the forces of the king. But before the sun was high, military companies from the adjoining towns began to arrive, and volunteers from all parts of Concord came, with such weapons as they could find, to increase the force, until the number had grown to two hundred and fifty or three hundred. Then, though greatly outnumbered by the British regulars, they "deliberately, with noble patriotism and firmness, resolved to march into the middle of the town to defend their homes, or die in the attempt; and, at the same time, they resolved not to fire unless first fired upon."

If they had known what had happened the day before at Lexington, they might have been less scrupulous. But their determination to make the British take the initiative in the fighting showed how coolly they were carrying themselves in the midst of all these exciting events. How steadily they marched down to the bridge, receiving first a few scattering shots of the British soldiery, and then a fierce volley that killed two of their men and wounded two others; how bravely they took up the gage of battle then, and drove the red coats from the bridge and from the town; how pluckily they dogged them all the way to Charlestown Neck, falling on their flanks as they hastily retreated, and making the road by which they marched a continual ambuscade;—all this has been told oftener than any other tale of our history; and it shall continue to kindle the patriotism of countless generations of brave boys yet unborn; till, by and by, it will pass that undiscovered bourne which divides history from mythology, and philosophers will forge elaborate treatises in languages yet unwritten, to prove that there never was any such war as the Revolutionary war, nor any such town as Concord, but that this story is only a type or illustration of the great struggle between Liberty and Authority which has been going on for so many ages. Let us all be thankful that we live in the day when the story is not a myth, but one of the solidest facts of history; and when we may read in this quiet field by the river side, on the marble inlet of the granite shaft that commemorates the day and the deed, these substantial statements:

"HERE, on the 19th of April, 1775, was made the first forcible resistance to British aggression. On the opposite banks stood the American militia. Here stood the invading army, and on this spot the first of the enemy fell in the war of the Revolution, which gave Independence to these United States. In gratitude to God, and in the love of Freedom this monument was erected, A. D. 1836."

Eighty-six years from this very day, in the city of Baltimore, on the 19th of April, 1861, the first soldier fell in the later and greater conflict which gave to the country the Liberty which the Declaration of Independence only promised, and consummated the work here begun. That first soldier was—it is almost a matter of course—a Massachusetts man; and his home was in this gallant old County of Middlesex in which we are standing now. If we walk back to the public square in the middle of the town, we shall find another granite shaft bearing witness in such words as these to the fact that Old Concord was ready to do her part in the last war as nobly as in the first:

"The town of Concord builds this monument in honor of the brave men whose names it bears, and records with grateful pride that they found here a birthplace, home or grave. They died for their country in the War of the Rebellion, 1861 to 1865."

And now that we are reading monumental inscriptions we may be minded to visit the old burial-places in this village, where many quaint epitaphs are found but none quainter than the following, many times published already, and so full of antithesis that Macaulay himself, if he ever read it, must have laid down his pen in despair of ever being able to match it:

> "God wills us free;—man wills us slaves. I will as God wills; God's will be done. Here lies the body of JOHN JACK, a native of Africa, who died, March, 1773, aged about sixty years. Though born in a land of slavery, he was born free. Though he lived in a land of liberty, he lived a slave; till by his honest, though stolen labors he acquired the source of slavery, which gave him his freedom; though not long before Death, the grand tyrant, gave him his final emancipation, and put him on a footing with kings. Though a slave to vice, he practised those virtues without which kings are but slaves."

Journeying westward again, through a region not remarkably picturesque, we halt for the first time at *South Acton*, where the Marlboro branch of the Fitchburg road diverges southward. While the train stops you get a pretty little view on the left, a pond in the foreground, and hills in the distance. From this town of Acton marched before day on the morning of the 19th of April, 1775, the two men made immortal at Concord by the first volley of the English soldiery,— Captain Isaac Davis, and Abner Hosmer.

West Acton is a neat hamlet, mainly on the south of the track.

Littleton is too small to be seen from the railroad, but not too small to be the scene of a large story about a certain lake, ominously called Nagog, where a strange rumbling noise is sometimes heard.

Groton Junction, a large and flourishing village a little further on, is the hub of which railroads running in six different directions are the spokes. The Fitchburg Railroad and the Worcester and Nashua Railroad pass *through* the town; the Stony Brook Railroad runs north-eastward to Lowell, and the Peterboro and Shirley Branch north-westward to Mason Village, in New Hampshire. The Indian name of the town was *Petapaway*, and its present name was probably given to it by one of the original grantees to whom the territory was conveyed by the General Court in 1655,—Mr. Dean Winthrop, son of Governor Winthrop. Groton was the home of the Winthrop family in England.

Shirley is a thrifty and presentable manufacturing town, of a few hundred inhabitants on the bank of a stream that empties into the Nashua River. About—this—time—look out—for—Shakers;—to borrow the method of the almanac. In Harvard, a few miles south, and in the town of Shirley, they have flourishing communities, and their broad brims and sober faces are commonly visible, at any of the stations in this neighborhood. In leaving Shirley we pass out of old Middlesex County, into Worcester County.

Lunenberg is the next station. Two or three miles beyond it, an extensive and beautiful view is opened to the southward. Leominster Center with its three church spires stands in the middle of a charming landscape, two or three miles away, and the hills in the horizon gave to the picture a majestic outline. This is one of the most distant, and on the whole the most satisfactory outlook we have had since leaving Boston. When the train stops at North Leominster, Wachusett Mountain is in full view, between two nearer hills.

Passing *North Leominster*, a young and ambitious village, called into existence by the railroad we are soon in the suburbs of

FITCHBURG.

This is the largest town we have seen since leaving Cambridge. It was incorporated in 1764, the region where it stands being known before that time by the name of *Turkey Hills*, from the large number of wild turkeys found there. At the time of the opening of the Fitchburg Railroad, in 1845, it was a smart little manufacturing village of something over three thousand inhabitants; and four hundred thousand dollars would buy all the goods and wares it produced in a year; now its population is not less than eleven thousand; its valuation is between six and seven millions of dollars, and more goods are manufactured every year than were manufactured in twenty years before the opening of the railroad.

This rapid growth of population and business has been largely the result of the increased railroad facilities. But for the railroad connecting it with Boston, Fitchburg would probably be a smaller town now than it was twenty-five years ago. When that railroad was projected, it was strongly opposed on the ground that there was not and would never be business enough to pay interest on the cost of construction. One of the legislators declared that "a six-horse coach and a few baggage wagons would draw all the freight from Fitchburg to Boston." Several six-horse coaches and quite a train of baggage wagons would be required to do the large business of this road to-day.

Fitchburg is not a stylish town. There is evidently very little aristocracy here. It is apparent that the people have not yet reached the point of giving much attention to matters of taste and elegance. Fitchburg means business. It impresses you as being a place of intense energy and vigor. It has some handsome churches,—notably the one recently built by the Episcopalians; it has several excellent school-houses,—in the year 1867 it expended seventy-five thousand dollars for new ones; it has a jail and house of correction that would prove, one would think, almost too attractive; it has one or two good hotels; it has many excellent houses; all the solid elements of the best civilization are here; but the people have, as yet, had but little time to give to architecture and landscape gardening. Æsthetical culture will soon follow, however; and the town will at length be made as picturesque as now it is plain and practical. These hillsides may, under skillful treatment, become a very Arcadia for loveliness.

The town is situated in a deep ravine, through which a branch of the Nashua river flows with rapid descent, affording, within the limits of the town, a distance of five miles, no less than twenty-eight excellent water-privileges. This power is all utilized. Here is the Putnam Machine Company, a mammoth establishment, making the Burleigh Rock Drill, which was invented in this town, and all sorts of iron work. This is only one of several machine-shops. Here are manufactories for building Mowing and Reaping Machines, and for making scythes and knives used in various agricultural implements. More than a thousand men find employment in these various foundries and machine-shops. Chair-making furnishes employment to about five hundred persons. Chairs are made, put together and painted, then knocked to pieces and boxed for shipping. The American Ratan Company gives employment to seventy-five persons. Ten paper-mills employ two hundred hands, and annually make three thousand five hundred tons of paper, worth at present prices one million of dollars. Three woolen-mills, three cotton-mills, and one factory making worsted yarn require for their operation nearly four hundred persons. Besides these, and many other things which cannot be mentioned, Fitchburg makes boots and shoes, palm-leaf hats and bonnets, reeds and harnesses for looms; wool cards; brass fixtures of various sorts; doors and sash; piano-cases,—*and* money. Nearly fifty different kinds of manufacturing are constantly in progress in this busy town. People who are interested in the industrial developments of the country could spend a day or two here with great profit to themselves. Neither is the region wanting in attractions for those who love the picturesque in nature.

Rollstone mountain, whose granite quarries supply the town with excellent building material, rises abruptly on the western side of the river to a height of three hundred feet. The view from its summit is worth climbing for. On the one side lie the village and the hills beyond; on the other you look across a beautiful country to Wachusett, ten miles distant,—the highest land in Eastern Massachusetts. Perhaps after you have viewed it from afar, you will conclude to go over and possess yourself of its glories. That you can easily do. The Vermont and Massachusetts Railroad will carry you to a station named Wachusett, where the stages will take you up and land you at the mountain. There you will find good hotels; the mountain top is easily accessible; and a day or two in that high and pure air will do you good. The top of this mountain is a little more than three thousand feet above tide water; and rises, without any very steep ascent, nearly two thousand feet above the surrounding country, of which it gives you a view from thirty to fifty miles in extent on every side.

Only three miles from Fitchburg is Pearl Hill—to the top of which good roads lead you, and from which you may count twenty villages. Perhaps too you may find the place where this thing happened, of which we read in Torrey's History of Fitchburg:

"On one occasion, Isaac Gibson in his rambles on Pearl Hill found a bear's cub, which he immediately seized as his legitimate prize. The mother of the cub came to the rescue of her offspring. Gibson retreated, and the bear attacked him in the rear, to the manifest detriment of his pantaloons. This finally compelled him to face his unwelcome antagonist and they closed in a more than fraternal embrace. Gibson, being the more skillful wrestler of the two, threw Bruin and they came to the ground together. Without relinquishing the hug both man and beast now rolled over each other to a considerable distance down the hill, receiving sundry bruises by the way. When they reached the bottom both were willing to relinquish the contest without any further experience of each others prowess. It was a draw game; the bear losing her cub, and Gibson his pantaloons."

Whether this was the contest upon which the wife looked, bestowing her applause so impartially upon both combatants, the historian does not tell us; but it is safe to assert that there are few *eastern* towns of the size of Fitchburg that can tell a bigger bear story.

Falloolah is the musical name of a pretty glen in the neighborhood, of which Mr. J. C. Moulton, the excellent photographer of Fitchburg will tell you, and a picture of which he will show you. Mr. Moulton is, by the way, an authority concerning all the points of interest about Fitchburg and visitors would do well to consult him. If they cannot visit all the places he can tell them of, they can possess themselves of some of his admirable stereographs. Not only Fitchburg and its surroundings but other neighborhoods are represented in his collection. A series of photographs of the Au Sable Chasm, in northern New York, gives a most satisfactory representation of one of the remarkable natural curiosities in America. Mention is made of this collection of stereographs in this place because they have been made with such excellent taste and skill, and are so well worth the notice of persons interested in this branch of art.

The Vermont and Massachusetts Railroad carries us westward from Fitchburg, through a rough country, over which we occasionally catch a glimpse to which distance lends enchantment. *Westminster Depot* is three miles from Westminster Village. The road from the railroad to the town is a pleasant one even in the winter, which is saying much for a country road; and must be well worth traveling in the summer. The old village to which it leads is a good specimen of a New England hill town. The only thing that astonishes the visitor is the architecture of some of the dwellings in the principal street, which have an air of tremendous boldness and self-assertion.

Ashburnham is remembered by all passengers as the place where their seats and their heads are turned. Here, for some unaccountable reason, there is a sharp angle in the railroad track. The train stops on a switch; the locomotive is turned round and attached to the rear end of the train, and you are soon going back, apparently in the direction from which you have come. A better route has just been surveyed, south of this line, from Gardner through Westminster to Fitchburg, by which the angle will be avoided, the distance shortened and the grade improved. The road will soon be built in accordance with this survey. From some of the elevated grades in this town you get fine views to the southward.

Gardner is a flourishing village four miles west of Ashburnham, to which the railroad has given a wonderful stimulus, though it has long been a town of considerable importance, owing to its extensive manufacture of chairs. Though a small village, it has the lead in this branch of industry of all the other towns in the Commonwealth. Not much is seen of the village from the railroad. It is hidden among the hills on the north of the track. This fact led a reckless passenger to remark that Gardner was a very *chary* town. It is to be hoped that he was immediately ejected from the car.

Just beyond Gardner the railroad crosses Miller's River, a considerable stream emptying into the Connecticut above Turner's Falls. The railroad follows the course of this river for the next forty miles, and from this point onward the scenery owes much of its attractiveness to the beauty of the river. Winding among the hills we meet a succession of picturesque surprises, which cannot be described or pointed out, but which the wide awake traveler will not be likely to miss.

Templeton lies to the southward of the track. This town, like Westminster, was an original grant to certain persons who did service in King Philip's war or to their heirs, and was known by the name of Narragansett No. 6 till 1762, when it was incorporated with the present name.

By this time the Pop-corn Man will have made his appearance. Johnson is his name, but he is a better looking and a much better natured man than the other Johnson. If you greet him with a gentle inclination of the head, he will stop by your side, take a paper bag of crisp and flaky corn from his capacious basket, shake a little salt into it from a small glass caster, deftly twirl it round once or twice in his fingers and pass it to you, discoursing all the time, in the most fluent manner, of "fate, free-will, foreknowledge absolute," or any other subject you choose to open, and charging you for paper bag, politeness, pop-corn and philosophy only five cents. Cultivate Johnson; he will tell you much more than this book knows about the country through which you are passing, and make you feel that you are doing him a favor in giving him an opportunity to answer questions.

Baldwinsville, a village in the town of Templeton, detains us but a moment, and soon after we leave it we have a fine view of Mount Monadnock in New Hampshire, ten miles to the north.

South Royalston is the village on the railroad—old Royalston being about five miles northward. Several pretty cascades in this vicinity are turned to good account for manufacturing purposes.

Athol is a lively and enterprising town, of three thousand inhabitants, on the western border of Worcester County,—another remarkable instance of the value of railroads in developing the resources of the country. Since the Vermont and Massachusetts Railroad was opened, this town has made remarkable progress; its excellent water-power is put to excellent use, and the wealth of the town has been trebled.

Orange is another village nearly as large, rivalling Athol in its activity and vigor. The manufacturing interest is large already, and is constantly increasing. Miller's River, which does the work of these smart villages gives to the traveler many beautiful glimpses of quiet pastoral beauty, as he hurries along its banks.

Wendell and *Erving* are feeling the impulse of the railroad also, and in due time they will no doubt grow into prominence and prosperity.

Grout's Corner is the terminus of the New London Northern Railroad, running southward through Amherst, Belchertown, Palmer and other important towns to New London in Connecticut. Here the Vermont and Massachusetts Railroad branches,—one track going north to Brattleboro, the other, which we shall follow, passing westward to Greenfield. Grout's Corner is making a commendable effort to live and thrive; and though it has tried once before and failed, all good people will wish it abundant success in its new endeavor. In this region there is abundance of charming scenery. A beautiful mountain view is seen to the northward, before reaching Grout's Corner,—blue hills in the distance, with a rolling country between. Just east of the depot, a deep and cool ravine gives a bed to Miller's River, from which we part at this point with regret, having found it for many miles a charming traveling companion. Two or three miles beyond Grout's Corner, a pretty little pond with wooded shores smiles in at the car windows on the northern side.

Montague is a fine old village, half a mile south of the railroad, and not visible from the cars. Soon after leaving the station which bears this name, the train emerges from a wooded bank upon a high, uncovered bridge, with the broad, clear current of the Connecticut flowing beneath, and the glorious valley opening like the Land of Promise to the northward and the southward. After so many miles of hills and cliffs and gorges, that tell of upheavals in the earth and forces primeval that have tossed and rent and piled the solid elements, how restful is the peace of this green valley with its circlet of blue hills! Away yonder on the right are the heights of Northfield and Bernardston; southward the symmetrical cones of the Sunderland hills; westward the rugged ridge of Rocky Mountain, over which the Shelburne Mountains lift their heads, and through which the Deerfield flows to its peaceful wedlock with the Connecticut; and all the wide interval is goodly and fruitful meadow land, green with grass or golden with grain. Quickly the train draws its smoky line across this beautiful picture; crosses the Deerfield; follows its path through the gorge it has cleft through Rocky Mountain; pauses for a moment that we may gaze upon a new vision of splendor in the smiling meadows of old Deerfield, then hurries on to the Greenfield station, where you and I, good reader, are to rest awhile.

"Free carriage to the Mansion House!" That means a good bed, a bountiful and sumptuous table, and a genial host. "Free carriage to the American House!" That tells of one who will give you abundant welcome and good cheer. Pay your money and take your choice! Rest and be thankful!

CHAPTER II.

GREENFIELD AND THEREABOUTS.

EARLY HISTORY.

THIS good town of Greenfield, which, for the next few days, will be our resting-place and base of operations, lies on the northern verge of the famous Deerfield meadows, in the angle between the Deerfield and Connecticut Rivers, whose waters unite two miles south-eastward from the Public Square. The Connecticut is hidden from the village by a greenstone ridge extending from Fall River on the north to South Deerfield, where it terminates in the well-known Sugar Loaf Mountain.

The town was originally a part of Deerfield, and was then called Green River. In 1753 it received its charter of incorporation. A dispute arose at this time concerning the boundary line between the towns, and concerning the use and improvement of certain sequestered lands, which has occasioned no little strife and litigation. In the courts and the Legislature the battle has been fought with great pertinacity; many hard words have been spoken and much printer's ink has been shed about it, and once, at least, it led to a slight unpleasantness with pitchforks between the farmers of the two different towns. The fact that these sequestered lands in dispute were for the use and behoof of the gospel ministry makes the quarrel slightly ridiculous if not disgraceful. No longer ago than 1850, the boundary question was before the Massachusetts Legislature, but if it has been mooted since that day this little book does not know of it.

The historic period of Greenfield was the early part of the eighteenth century, while it was yet a part of Deerfield; and when we come to trace the story of Indian wars and incursions our path will frequently cross this territory. In the War of the Revolution, however, this town bore an honorable part.

"When the news of the battle of Lexington reached Greenfield, the people assembled on the afternoon of the same day, and formed a company of volunteers on the spot choosing Benjamin Hastings captain. Hastings, however became himself second in command, yielding the first rank to Captain Timothy Childs, who, he modestly said, was a man of greater experience than himself. Aaron Davis was then chosen ensign, and the next morning the company marched for Cambridge. During the whole War of the Revolution the people of this town took an active interest in its progress and success, as is abundantly shown by the numerous records of votes choosing committees of correspondence and safety, approving the confederation of the United States, raising money for ammunition and food, and hiring men for the army, as well as by their prompt personal obedience to the calls for re-enforcements."*

WAR RECORD.

The spirit of '76 again took possession of the people of Greenfield in 1861 when President Lincoln's first call for troops was issued. Once more the bells were rung, and the people assembled, eager to buckle on the armor that their fathers had so nobly worn. From one manufacturing establishment an entire company volunteered, and the quota was speedily in marching order. In the last war as well as in the first Greenfield has a full and honorable record.

CHURCHES AND PUBLIC BUILDINGS.

Going forth from our comfortable quarters at the Mansion House or the American Hotel we find ourselves upon the Main street of the village. Nearly opposite the Mansion House is the Public Square, an oblong space of half an acre surrounded by a low wooden railing. The town has recently voted to build an iron fence and to erect a Soldiers' Monument. The most conspicuous object on the north side of the square is the Orthodox Congregational Church, now building of red sandstone. The symmetry and the solidity of the structure are the admiration of visitors and the pride of the inhabitants.

The first minister of Greenfield was Rev. Edward

* Holland's Western Massachusetts: Vol. II., p. 371.

Billings, settled September 24, 1753. The first meeting-house was built in 1760, about a mile north of the village on the Bernardston road. Soon after the meeting-house was built Rev. Roger Newton was ordained as pastor of the church and continued in this office until 1816, when he died at the age of 79, having had but this one pastorate of fifty-six years. During the last three years of his ministry he had for his colleague Rev. Gamaliel S. Olds, afterwards for a long time professor of mathematics in Vermont University and in Amherst College. In 1817 the church was divided; and the Second Society erected its new edifice in 1819 on the ground where the present church is building. The old meeting-house stood until 1831 when it was taken down and a new one was built by the First Society at Nash's Mills three-quarters of a mile west of the old site.

The Rev. Dan Huntington, the father of the Rev. Frederick Dan Huntington, D. D., recently of Boston and now bishop of Central New York preached for the Second Society for some time after its organization, though he was never settled as its pastor. The name of Rev. P. C. Headley, well-known in literature, is found among the recent ministers of this church. Rev. Samuel H. Lee is the present pastor.

The Unitarian Church whose edifice is just above on the opposite side of Main street was organized in 1825. Its first minister was Rev. Winthrop Bailey, and its present pastor is Rev. John F. Moors.

The Episcopal Church was organized in 1812. Its

excellent house of worship stands on Federal street, Rev. P. V. Finch is the rector.

The Methodist Church was organized in 1835. You notice its edifice on Church street, north of Main.

The Baptist Church, organized in 1852 and ministered to at present by Rev. D. M. Grant, has its local habitation on Main street west of the Square.

The Roman Catholic Church, whose pastor is Rev. Mr. Robinson, is about to erect a new church on Main street.

People stopping in Greenfield over Sunday may therefore even if they are not, like Mrs. Partington, so Catholic in their sentiments as to be satisfied with "any paradox church where the gospel is dispensed with," find a place of worship where their preferences will be gratified.

Next door to the Orthodox Church, on the Public Square, stands the Court House,—Greenfield being the shire town of Franklin County. The contiguity of these two edifices is suggestive, and a short intermission will be given, at this point, to all those persons who want to go out and make puns about them.

On the eastern side of the Square is the Post Office, and just below the Square, on the south side of Main street, is the Town Hall, a fine brick structure. The Jail, standing on a side street south-east from the Square, is one of the best buildings in town. On Chapman street is the High School, and on Federal street the Greenfield Institute for Young Ladies, under the care of the Misses Stone,—an institution which for many years has borne an excellent name. The education of the young probably costs more than it did in 1753, when this town voted to pay teachers two shillings a day for the summer and one shilling and fourpence for the fall.

Some members of the illustrious Gradgrind family are always found in every company of tourists. They do not approve of mountains and waterfalls, but they would enjoy a visit to an establishment which has not only a national, but an European reputation,—

THE RUSSELL MANUFACTURING COMPANY.

Up to the year 1841, the table cutlery used in the United States was almost all of English manufacture. No competition with the great Sheffield manufactories had been attempted, and it was supposed that such an attempt would not be successful. But in that year, Mr. John Russell, who for seven years had been manufacturing edge tools on the Green River, in this village, and who had during this time made some table cutlery with considerable success, resolved to turn his attention to the exclusive manufacture of the latter class of goods. From that beginning has grown this large establishment,—the largest of its class in the world, making cutlery which the Sheffield manufacturers confess to be superior to theirs, and affording it at prices so reasonable that it controls the American market. This result has been attained by the superior mechanical skill and inventive genius of Mr. Russell and those who have wrought with him. Many curious machines, by which the labor of production is greatly facilitated, were invented here, and are not found in operation elsewhere. Almost all the work of these shops is done by machinery; and low as are the wages of Sheffield mechanics, the Yankee machines will work cheaper and better than they. Moreover, the machines are never known to go off "on a tear," and though some of them strike pretty frequently, the work never stops on that account.

"Among these curious machines is an arrangement of screw-frames and heated dies for the purpose of giving form and hardness to the apple-wood handles which are put upon some styles of knives. The comparatively soft apple-wood, by being thus subjected to an immense pressure, is made to take the place of ebony, rosewood, cocoa or granadilla wood; at the same time the brass rivets are headed, and a beautiful handle is the result. By an ingenious arrangement of circular saws and endless chains, a machine has been contrived for the purpose of sawing out bone and ivory handles as fast as a man can clap the pieces on the machine. Another instrument drills the holes in the handles; another one cuts the tines of the forks; another bends the tines to their proper shape; another straightens and levels the blade of the knife at one stroke; still another cuts the blade from the piece of steel which has been formed ready for use."*

Nearly all the forging is done by steam. Twelve

* *New York Evening Mail.* This quotation, and many of the facts here presented, were taken from an article in that newspaper.

trip-hammers make titanic music all day long. In the grinding and polishing shops, whose flooring is about half an acre in extent, one hundred and forty grinders are at work upon seventy grindstones; and there are one hundred men employed on the emery wheels. These wheels are made of wood, covered with leather, dressed with wax, and rolled in emery dust. The emery is of various grades of fineness; the coarsest, which is used for grinding the wooden handle, being in grains as large as coarse meal or hominy, the finest, which is used only for polishing, being fine as flour.

One building is devoted to the tempering of the knives. The blade is first heated red hot and dipped into oil; this makes it exceedingly brittle. It is then laid upon iron plates covered with sand over a coal fire, and the heat changes the color first to gray, then to straw color, then to pink, then to blue. The workman judges of the temper by his eye. One man can temper about twenty-five hundred blades in a day.

The new silver-plated knife, with both handle and blade of steel, is made at these works.

The Green River supplies three water-wheels with one hundred and twenty-five horse power; two steam engines, with a total of three hundred and fifty horse power, do the rest of the work. Five hundred men and twenty women earn a little more than twenty thousand dollars a month.

England and America supply this company annually with six hundred tons of steel; the West Indies contribute three hundred thousand pounds of cocoa and granadilla wood; California sends sixty thousand pounds of rose-wood; Madagascar a hundred thousand pounds of ebony; Africa forty thousand pounds of elephants' tusks; Smyrna fifty thousand pounds of emery; Nova Scotia four hundred thousand pounds of grindstones; Connecticut thirty thousand pounds of brass wire; Pennsylvania two thousand tons of anthracite coal; Massachusetts and Vermont twenty-five thousand bushels of charcoal; and the Yankee bees, who are not less busy than other bees, have a yearly contract for supplying twenty-five hundred pounds of wax.

With this material, the Green River Works turn out every day one thousand dozen of table cutlery, one hundred dozen ivory-handled ware, and two hundred and fifty dozen of miscellaneous goods.

Of the other manufacturing establishments of Greenfield we cannot speak at length. We have tarried long enough among the things that man has made. Let us go and look at the house of a better Builder. Being a little weary with car-riding, we propose to rest ourselves with a walk, this fine evening, to look upon the landscape and enjoy the sunset from

THE POET'S SEAT.

Up Main street under a canopy of elms and maples, to the end of the street where a guide-board points us into a road leading to Montague, bearing to the right, and passing round the elegant residence of Judge Grinnell. The highway winding up the hill gives us some glimpses of scenery, but prudently keeps from us the glories to be revealed when we reach the top. There, at the summit, we turn to the left, into a bushy pasture, and suddenly the landscape is unveiled. We are standing now on Rocky Mountain, looking eastward; the Deerfield Valley, out of which we have ascended, is behind us, and is hidden from view by the hill, over the crest of which we have passed; the Connecticut River and its valley are before us. A little way to the south the Deerfield River breaks through the ridge on which we are standing and flows down through the meadow to mingle its waters with those of the Connecticut. To the northward we catch a glimpse of Turner's Falls, and the racing rapids below them; across the valley to the north-eastward in the distant horizon rises Mount Grace in the town of Warwick;—southward is Mount Toby in Sunderland; other lesser eminences complete the horizon, and encircle a scene most fair. Directly across the river is Montague City, reached by the bridge which spans the Connecticut at this point and greatly adds to the beauty of the picture. On the little island at our feet a musket was dug up not long ago, which may very likely have belonged to one of those Indians who went down the rapids in the Falls fight, about which we shall know more by and by. In the meadow just below us is a sulphur spring the water of which tastes bad enough to be very medicinal. Good Mr. Philo Temple, who owns the meadow says that the spring has had its ups and downs for a hundred and fifty years; sometimes being highly extolled for its healing virtues and sometimes entirely neglected. Just now it is out of fashion, and therefore we will give it none of our patronage.

When you have rested and feasted your eyes upon this landscape long enough, we will turn into this well-trodden path running northward along the Ridge, keeping the same prospect in view for a third of a mile, when the path passes over the crest and opens to us another scene scarcely less beautiful, on the western side of the Ridge. On the brink of this steep, rocky wall, where we are standing, is the niche in the rock long known as the Poet's Seat. It is not generally supposed, in the neighborhood of Greenfield, that all the people who have sat in this seat are poets, or that sitting here is sure to make a poet out of a common man; however, if any one chooses to try it, there is no impediment. No one but a poet ought to attempt to describe the vision which is here brought before us. At our feet Greenfield and the valley of the Green River, flanked by the hills of Leyden and Shelburne; to the south Old Deerfield, hidden among its elms; over against it, in the boundary between Deerfield and Conway, Arthur's Seat, a noble mountain; in the middle of the picture the enchanting meadows of the Deerfield, with their many-figured, many-tinted carpeting. Upon this sloping bank let us sit down, while the shadows creep stealthily, as once the red man crept, eastward across the valley at our feet; while the clouds above the Shelburne hills change to gold and amber and crimson and purple; while the robin in the branches overhead sings his vesper song, and the evening star shines out in the west; then silently, as the twilight fades, we will rise and seek the path that will lead us quickly down from this mount of beautiful vision.

> "Black shadows fall
> From the lindens tall
> That lift aloft their massive wall
>   Against the southern sky;
>
> "And from the realms
> Of the shadowy elms,
> A tide-like darkness overwhelms
>   The fields that round us lie.
>
> "But the night is fair,
> And everywhere
> A warm soft vapor fills the air,
>   And distant sounds seem near;
>
> "And above, in the light
> Of the star-lit night,
> Swift birds of passage wing their flight
>   Through the dewy atmosphere."

We went, as was meet, to the Poet's Seat last eventide; this morning a place with a name something less romantic will be the destination of our walk:

THE BEAR'S DEN.

We follow Main street again to the end, turn again into the Montague road, and a few rods beyond the residence of Judge Grinnell we take a well-trodden path, which leads through a beautiful pasture on the right of the highway. Following this path for about a mile, with a bright panorama nearly all the while in view, we come to the southern end of Rocky Mountain, where the Deerfield River pierces the barrier and descends into the Connecticut Valley. Tradition says that this Deerfield Valley was once a lake brimful of water to the top of this hill, and that a squaw, with a clam-shell, scraped away the earth at this point for the water to flow over into the Connecticut Valley, thus opening a channel which the water has worn till it has cut the mountain in two and emptied the lake. Undoubtedly the valley was once a lake, and the water has worn this channel; but the squaw and her clam-shell are mildly apocryphal. This is not the only place where they have done duty. The same story is told, unless we forget, of the parting between Tom and Holyoke through which the Connecticut River runs; and upon the banks of every old water basin in the land that has been drained, tradition has perched the same old squaw with her clam-shell. Standing at this point, both valleys are seen, and the view is beautiful in both directions. The wagon-bridge, which crosses the Deerfield River just above us, was built as a toll-bridge in 1798, and its charter ran seventy years; in November, 1868, it became free, and passed into the possession of the town of Deerfield.

The railroad bridge, which stands above it, by which the Connecticut River Railroad crosses the Deerfield River, is seven hundred and fifty feet in length, and ninety feet above the water. On the morning of July

17, 1864, during the draft riots, the bridge which stood where this one stands was burnt,—with what purpose is not quite clear. It was supposed at the time that the object was to call the people and the fire department away from Greenfield, when the town was to have been set on fire. If this was the intent of the incendiary, he failed in his purpose, for the citizens stood by their own stuff, and let the bridge burn.

The Bear's Den is a rough and steep ravine with a sort of cavern at the southern extremity of this hill, up which ardent and adventurous youth sometimes clamber. Sitting in the Poet's Seat will not make a man a poet, but climbing up the Bear's Den is very likely to make a man as hungry as a bear. If any one lacks appetite, therefore, let him make the experiment; while those of us who do not need this kind of sharpening will at once descend to dinner.

Those who are not vigorous enough to make these longer tramps of which we have been talking will find it a pleasant walk to the end of Congress street, leading directly south from the head of Main street. The western view from this point is very beautiful.

The drives about Greenfield are no less inviting than the walks, and first among them for interest is the drive to

OLD DEERFIELD.

In order that we may fully appreciate the scenes upon which we shall look, we will study for a little while, before we start, the early history of this famous old town. Originally Deerfield embraced within its limits the present towns of Conway, Shelburne, Greenfield and Gill; and its settlement was on this wise. Eliot, the celebrated Indian apostle, after some years of labor among the red men, reached a conclusion not unlike that which has lately found expression in the President's Message,—that civilization and citizenship were indispensable to the Christianization of the Indians. He therefore in 1651 asked the General Court for two thousand acres of land at Natick, then a part of Dedham, upon which he might found an Indian community. This reasonable request was granted. As a recompense for the lands thus taken away the General Court in 1663 voted that the town of Dedham might select for itself eight thousand acres of unoccupied land anywhere within the province. In the same year messengers were sent out to locate the land. They traveled as far west as Lancaster, to the Chestnut Hills; and very likely climbed to the top of Wachusett, from which the country was visible for many miles on either side. They returned and reported that the land was rough and uneven, offering few inducements to pioneers. The next spring an old hunter told the people of Dedham that there was land worth possessing on the Connecticut River, north of Hadley. Immediately they appointed one of their number to go with him and spy out the land. The report they brought back was so favorable that four men were commissioned to proceed to the spot and locate the land. They journeyed westward through the unbroken forest, till they reached the Connecticut

Valley which they crossed not far below the mouth of the Deerfield, and climbed to the top of the rocky ridge separating the two valleys, when a scene was presented to their eyes fairer than any they had beheld on this Continent. The wide valley then as now was green with verdure; no forests had grown since the ancient lake was drained; the course of the Deerfield was marked by thickets that grew upon its banks; thousands of acres of smooth and fruitful land rudely planted by the red man were waiting for a better cultivation. No wonder that these good Puritans gave vent to their joy in fervent and Scriptural thanksgiving. They at once proceeded to locate their eight thousand acres with excellent judgment, selecting what proved to be the best land in the region. Shortly thereafter, Major Pynchon of Springfield purchased this land of the Indians for the people of Dedham, paying therefor £94, 10*s*. The deeds by which the property was originally conveyed are now in the archives of the town of Deerfield. The date of the first settlement is not quite certain. It has commonly been fixed at 1671 or 1672; but some of the later students of the old history are inclined to place it as far back as 1669;—just two hundred years ago. At this time the only settlements of white men in this region were those of Hadley, Hatfield, Northampton and Springfield. Until the year 1675 these settlers dwelt in peace and security; then began the long train of conflicts and calamities which has no parallel in the pioneer history of any community in our country.

Massasoit, the Indian sachem who welcomed the Pilgrims to Plymouth, and proved himself, during his whole life, a trusty friend of the white man, was succeeded by his son Philip, a chief of a very different temper. Perceiving that the English were gaining rapidly in numbers and influence, and that the empire of the red man was in danger, he formed the various Indian tribes of New England into an alliance for the purpose of exterminating the whites. Hostilities began in the year 1675; and the first serious contest in Western Massachusetts was in Brookfield, in July of that year, where an ambuscade, a siege and a conflagration signalized the ferocity of the savages. The Pocumtuck Indians, whose hunting grounds were in this valley, at first professed hostility to Philip; but shortly after the siege of Brookfield, the wily sachem found his way into this region, and won their allegiance. At this time Hadley was the head-quarters of the English forces, and about one hundred and eighty men were then in garrison, under Captains Beers and Lathrop. The treachery of the Indians in this vicinity being suspected, they were ordered to deliver up their arms. This they promised to do; but on the night of the 25th of August, before their arms had been given up, they secretly left their quarters and fled up the river. Beers and Lathrop pursued them the next day, overtook and attacked them in South Deerfield, near the base of Sugar Loaf Mountain, and killed twenty-six of them, the remainder making good their escape to the camp of Philip, which was somewhere in the vicinity.

Ten of the English soldiers fell in this battle. One week afterward the Indians attacked the settlers in Deerfield, killed one of them, and burnt nearly all the houses in the little settlement. This was the 1st of September, 1675. But the settlement was not abandoned. A garrison was established here, and Captain Mosely was made Commandant. In the fields around Deerfield a large amount of wheat had been harvested and stacked. The winter was approaching, and this wheat must be secured before the Indians destroyed it. Accordingly, Captain Lathrop, with eighty soldiers and a large number of teams and drivers, were sent to thrash the grain and bring it to Hadley. They proceeded to Deerfield, thrashed and loaded the grain without molestation, and the 18th of September began their return march to Hadley. The rest of the story shall be told by General Hoyt, whose valuable History of the Indian Wars, now out of print, is the standard authority upon the early history of this region:—

"For the distance of about three miles after leaving Deerfield Meadow, Lathrop's march lay through a very level country, closely wooded, where he was every moment exposed to an attack on either flank. At the termination of this distance, near the south point of *Sugar Loaf Hill*, the road approximated Connecticut River, and the left was in some measure protected. At the village now called *Muddy Brook*, in the southerly part of Deerfield, the road crossed a small stream, bordered by a narrow morass, from which the village has its name; though, more appropriately, it should be denominated *Bloody Brook*, by which it was for some time known.* Before arriving at the point of intersection with the brook, the road for about half a mile ran parallel to the morass, then crossing it continued to the south point of Sugar Loaf Hill, traversing what is now the home-lots on the east side of the village. As the morass was thickly covered with brush, this place of crossing afforded a favorable point for surprise.

"On discovering Lathrop's march, a body of upwards of seven hundred Indians † planted themselves in ambuscade at this point, and lay eagerly waiting to pounce upon him while passing the morass. Without scouring the woods in his front and flanks, or suspecting the snare laid for him, Lathrop arrived at the fatal spot; crossed the morass with the principal part of his force, and probably halted to allow time for his teams to drag through their loads. The critical moment had arrived. The Indians instantly poured a heavy and destructive fire upon the column and rushed furiously to close attack. Confusion and dismay succeeded. The troops broke and scattered, fiercely pursued by the Indians whose great superiority [in numbers] enabled them to attack at all points. Hopeless was the situation of the scattered troops, and they resolved to sell their lives in a vigorous struggle. Covering themselves with trees the bloody conflict now became

* This suggestion of General Hoyt was adopted, and the stream is now known as Bloody Brook.

† Probably commanded by Philip himself.

a severe trial of skill in sharp shooting, in which life was the *stake.* Difficult would it be to describe the havoc, barbarity and misery that ensued; 'Fury raged, and shuddering pity quit the sanguine field,' while desperation stood pitted, 'at fearful odds' to unrelenting ferocity. The dead, the dying, the wounded strewed the ground in all directions, and Lathrop's devoted force was soon reduced to a small number, and resistance became faint. At length the unequal struggle terminated in the annihilation of nearly the whole of the English; only seven or eight escaped from the bloody scene to relate the dismal tale, and the wounded were indiscriminately butchered. Captain Lathrop fell in the early part of the action; the whole loss, including teamsters, amounted to ninety. The company was a choice corps of young men from the county of Essex in Massachusetts; many from the most respectable families. Hubbard says 'they were the flower of the county; none of whom were ashamed to speak with the enemy in the gate.' Captain Lathrop was from Salem, Massachusetts.

"Captain Mosely, at Deerfield, between four and five miles distant, hearing the musketry, made a rapid march for the relief of Lathrop, and arriving at the close of the struggle found the Indians stripping and mangling the dead. Promptly rushing on, in compact order, he broke through the enemy, and charging back and forth, cut down all within the range of his shot; and at length drove the remainder through the adjacent swamp, and another farther west, and after several hours of gallant fighting compelled them to seek safety in the more distant forests.

"Just at the close of the action, Major Treat (then commanding the garrison at Hadley,) who, on the morning of the day, had marched toward Northfield, arrived on the ground with one hundred men, and shared in the final pursuit of the enemy. The gallant Mosely lost but two men in the various attacks, and seven or eight only were wounded. Probably the Indians had expended most of their ammunition in the action with Lathrop, and occasionally fought with their bows and spears."

That night Mosely and Treat, with their men, slept in the garrison at Deerfield, and the next morning they returned to bury their dead. The number of Indians killed in the two engagements was ninety-six.

Shortly after this, it became evident that the post of Deerfield could only be held with the greatest difficulty. The garrison was therefore withdrawn to Hadley, and what was left of the little town was entirely destroyed by the savages.

It is not quite certain at what date the settlers returned to rebuild the ruined village. Philip's War continued till the spring of 1678, when a peace was concluded; but the power of the red men was broken in the Connecticut Valley at an earlier date. In the autumn of 1677, we find the people erecting dwellings and preparing for the coming winter. On the 19th of September, in that year, a party of about fifty Indians, who had descended the Connecticut River from Canada, and had made a successful assault upon the garrison of Hatfield, halted on their return in the woods east of Deerfield, entered the town about night-fall, killed one man and captured three others, whom they took with them to Canada. This calamity alarmed the good people of Deerfield, and they again deserted their plantation. But after the fall of Philip and the conclusion of peace, the Indians abandoned the territory, and the whites were left for a time in undisturbed possession.

Ten years of peace were now granted to the distracted settlers of the Connecticut Valley. These fruitful meadows of the Deerfield again gave seed to the sower and bread to the eater; the village was rebuilt, and the people began to hope that their calamities were past. But in the year 1689, the accession of William and Mary to the throne of England was followed by that war between England and France known in these colonies as King William's War. The gage of battle was taken up by the French and English colonists of North America; and the settlers of this region were again for five years harassed by constant apprehensions of attack from the French and their allies, the Indians. Several slight skirmishes with the Indians took place, but no very severe calamity befell the little town during this war, which closed with the peace of Ryswick, in 1691. In 1689 a fort was built, doubtless as a defence against expected incursions of the savages. This was a stockaded enclosure, more than two hundred rods in circumference, and containing about fifteen acres. Somewhere within this enclosure, the boundaries of which we can fix with some degree of certainty as we ride through the village, stood the first meeting-house, built probably of logs. October 30, 1694, we find the town voting,

"That a Meeting-House shall be built ye bignesse of Hatfield Meeting-House, only ye height to be left to ye judgment and determination of ye Committy.

"That there shall be a rate made of one hundred and forty pounds, payable the present year in Pork and Indian Corn, in equall proportions, for ye carrying on ye building."

Not only religion, but education was the earliest care of these wise pioneers. The next year this vote is recorded:

"That a school-house be built upon the town charge in ye year 1695, ye dimensions of said house to be 21 foot long and 18 foot wide and 7 between joynts."

The school-house and the meeting-house both stood within the limits of the fort.

The democracy of these days was by no means the most radical variety, as the following votes in town-meeting bear witness:—

"May 11, 1701, Voted that Dea. Hunt, Dea. Sheldon, Mr. John Catlen, Edward Allyn and Thomas French, shall be ye seaters for ye seating of ye new Meeting-House. That ye rules for ye seating of persons shall be Age, State and Dignity.

"Oct. 2, 1701, Voted that ye fore seats in ye front Gallery shall be equal in Dignity with ye 2nd seat in ye body of ye Meeting-House.

"That ye fore seats in ye side Gallery be equal with ye 4th seats in ye Body of ye Meeting-House.

"That ye 2nd seat in ye front Gallery and ye hinder seat in ye front Gallery shall be equal in Dignity with ye 5th seat in ye Body.

"That ye second seat in ye side Gallery shall be esteemed equal in Dignity with ye 6th in ye Body of the Meeting-House."

The minister at this time was Rev. John Williams, a graduate of Harvard College, who was settled in 1686, being then in his twenty-second year. The following is the agreement between him and his people, copied from the early records of the town:—

"The inhabitants of Deerfield, to encourage Mr. John Williams to settle amongst them to dispense the blessed word of truth unto them, have made propositions unto him as followeth:—

"That they will give him sixteen cow commons of meadow land, with a house lot that lyeth on the meeting-house hill; that they will build him a house forty-two feet long, twenty feet wide, with a lento on the back side of the house; to finish said house, to fence his home-lot, and within two year after this agreement to build him a barn and break up his plowing land. For yearly salary to give him sixty pounds a year for the present, and four or five years after this agreement to add to his salary and make it eighty pounds."

There was a further agreement between Mr. Williams and the town relative to his salary in 1696, the terms of which we find recorded by Mr. Williams himself:—

"The town to pay their salary to me in wheat, pease, Indian corn, and pork at the price stated, viz: wheat at 3s. 3d. per bushel, Indian corn at 2s. per bushel, fatted pork at 2d. 1-2 per lb.; these being the terms of the bargain made with me at the first.

(Signed) "JOHN WILLIAMS."

These old records illustrate for us the life of the early settlers during the years of comparative peace and plenty which closed the seventeenth century; and they show that the village, though annoyed by the war, was hardly interrupted in its growth. On the death of King William and the accession of Queen Anne, in 1702, another war broke out between England and France, which brought to these good people of Deerfield hardships greater than any they had yet suffered. At this time Deerfield had grown to be quite a village; there must have been a population of between two and three hundred souls, and several comfortable framed houses had been built, both within and without the fort. Deerfield was the frontier town on the north, the few inhabitants of Northfield having been driven from their homes during King William's War. On the breaking out of Queen Anne's War, in 1702, the purpose of the French to sack this town was discovered; the fort was repaired by the inhabitants, and twenty soldiers were sent by the Governor as a guard.

And now the last and worst of their calamities was ready to be visited upon them. On the night of the twenty-ninth of February 1704, Major Hertel de Rouville, with sixteen hundred French and one hundred and forty Indians, arrived at what is now known as Pettis' Plain,—a short distance south-west from the village of Greenfield, and two miles from the fort at Deerfield, having made a toilsome march of between two and three hundred miles, through a deep snow. Here he halted, ordered his men to lay aside their packs and snow-shoes, and prepare for an assault upon the fort. Crossing the Deerfield River a little before daybreak, he took up a rapid march on the stiff crust of the snow across the meadow. Fearing that the noise of the marching might give the alarm, he ordered frequent halts, in which the whole force lay still for a few moments, and then rising, rushed on at the double quick. These alternations of noise and silence, would he supposed, be mistaken by the sentinels for gusts of wind followed by moments of calm. It was a clever ruse, but hardly necessary, for the sentinels were asleep. On the north-west corner of the fort the snow had been drifted nearly to the top of the stockade, and over the bridge thus provided for them the whole force gained an easy entrance, and found the whole garrison asleep. Quietly they now divided themselves into parties, and began the assault. The doors were broken open, the people were dragged from their beds, and all who offered resistance were slaughtered.

The house of Mr. Williams was one of the first assaulted. Awakened from a sound sleep he sprang from his bed and ran toward the door, but the Indians had already entered. Quickly returning to his couch he seized a pistol there secreted, and aimed it at the foremost Indian, but it missed fire. Instantly he was seized and pinioned, and made to await the brutal pleasure of his captors. Two of his young children and his negro woman were taken to the door and murdered before his eyes. His wife and five children were made captives with him.

The door of Captain John Sheldon's house was so securely fastened that they could not force it open. With their hatchets they succeeded in cutting a small hole through the double thickness of plank, and thrusting a musket through they fired and killed Mrs. Sheldon who was just rising from her bed. The house was captured and used as a place of confinement for the prisoners. Another house about fifty yards south-west of Sheldon's was repeatedly attacked but was defended by seven men who poured a destructive fire from windows and loop-holes. The bullets that kept the foe at bay were cast by brave women while the fight was going on; a fact which Lucy Stone may use with excellent effect when she makes her next speech in the Connecticut Valley.

Another house outside the fort, surrounded by a circle of palisades, was successfully defended, with some loss to the assailants.

Before eight o'clock in the morning, the work of destruction and pillage was complete, and Rouville collected his prisoners and his booty, and set out on his return. Possibly his steps were hastened by the arrival of a party from Hatfield, whither the news of the assault had been carried by a fugitive. This small and late re-enforcement, being joined by the people who had defended the two houses, and a few others who had escaped into the woods, pursued the enemy into the meadow, and gallantly attacked them; but being outnumbered and almost surrounded, they were compelled to retreat, and the invaders marched away with their captives and their plunder. One hundred and twelve persons of both sexes and all ages were made prisoners; the slain, including those who fell in the fight in the meadows, numbered forty-seven, and the loss of the enemy was about the same number. Fourteen of the captives,—probably infants and infirm persons,—were killed by the Indians during the first day's march, which was not more than four miles. Two of them escaped, and Mr. Williams was instructed to inform the prisoners that if any more escapes were attempted, death by fire would be the portion of the rest. A full and graphic account of this sad journey, and the exile in Canada which succeeded it, may be found in a little book written by Mr. Williams, and entitled, "The Redeemed Captive Returning to Zion." The first day, he tells us, he was separated from his wife, who was in feeble health; the second day he was permitted to speak with her, and for a time to assist her on her journey; but at length her strength failed, and he was forced to leave her behind. The Indian to whose tender mercies she was left, finding her unable to travel further, despatched her with his tomahawk. Not long after, a party from Deerfield, following the trail of the Indians, found her dead body, and brought it back to Deerfield and buried it. By slow and weary marches through the deep snow, the prisoners finally arrived in Canada. It appears that they were regarded as the property of their Indian captors; and though some of them were purchased by the French inhabitants, the greater part were retained by the Indians at their lodges in different parts of the country. Mr. Williams was set at liberty by Governor Vaudreuil, and by great exertions succeeded in procuring the release of all his children but one, Eunice, a girl of ten years. In 1706 a flag-ship, sent from Boston to Quebec, returned with Mr. Williams, four of his children and fifty-two other redeemed captives. Eunice Williams was left behind, grew up among the Indians, forgot her language, married an Indian who assumed her name, reared up a large family, and died at length a Romanist in an Indian cabin. Three times during her life, attended by her tawny spouse, and attired in Indian costume, she visited her friends in Massachusetts; but they could not persuade her to forsake her home or to forswear her faith. Eleazer Williams, the pretended Dauphin of France, was her grandson.

The little party that bravely followed and assailed the invaders, found, on returning to the smoking ruins of the little village, that not much of it was left. Hoyt tells us that, "excepting the meeting-house and Sheldon's, which was the last fired, and saved by the English who assembled immediately after the enemy left the place all [the buildings] within the fort were consumed by fire. That which was so bravely defended by the seven men accidentally took fire and was consumed while they were engaged in the meadow." But this statement is now disputed. It is supposed that seven or eight houses remained after the burning, and some of them are yet standing. We shall see them as we ride through the village.

The house of Sheldon stood with but little alteration until 1849, when it was removed to make way for a more modern structure. The old door, which the Indians pierced with their tomahawks was still upon its hinges when the house was taken down, and it was preserved as a relic by Mr. Hoyt, the owner of the house. Some years afterward it passed into other hands, and at length in 1863, the citizens of the town learned with great regret that it had been purchased and carried away to Newton, by Dr. D. D. Slade. Negotiations were immediately opened with the worthy doctor, who at first refused to part with it; but finally, in 1867, he wrote to the committee that after thinking the matter over he had concluded that the door belonged to Deerfield; and upon receipt of the amount which it had cost him, he would return it to the town. Whereupon, a fair was held, the money was raised, and the people celebrated the return of the door with a festival, a speech by Rev. J. F. Moors of Greenfield, and a poem by Josiah D. Canning, Esq., of Gill, well known in this region as the "Peasant Bard." Here are some of his verses:

"Here where you stood in those dark days of yore,
And did brave duty as a *Bolted Door;*
Where you withstood the Indians' fiendish rage
Who on yon tablet, scored a bloody page;
Where you survived the havoc and the flame,
And float Time's tide to-day, a *Door of Fame;*
Here where for long decades of years gone down
You've served attractor to this grand old Town,
Made for yourself and physics one name more,—
For thou hast been, shalt be, *Attraction's Door;*

Here where years since, a wonder-loving boy,
I first beheld thee with a solemn joy,
Gazed on thy silent face but speaking scars,
And dreamed of "auld lang syne" and Indian wars;
Door of the Past, thou wast indeed to me
And *Door of Deerfield* thou shalt ever be!
Here grim old relic! thou shalt aye repose,
By keepers guarded, unassailed by foes;
Stronger in age than most doors in their prime,
The Indian's hatchet and the scythe of Time
Thou hast defied; and though no more for harm,
'Gainst thee the painted warrior nerves his arm,
Still shalt defy the blade of Time so keen,
Till he his scythe shall change for the *machine*.
"Bless thee, old relic! old and brave and scar'd!
And bless Old Deerfield! says her grandson bard.
Towns may traditions have, by error spun,
She has the *Door of History*,—here's the one!"

The old door is now enclosed in a handsome chestnut frame, and hung in the hall of the Pocumtuck House, where it is easily accessible to visitors: but it might find a better resting-place. Deerfield ought to have a Memorial Hall, into which its relics and its archives might be gathered. A large and valuable collection would soon be obtained; no town in the country, except Old Plymouth, has greater need of such a building. Some of the rich men of the cities, whose genealogical tree sprouted in these historic meadows, ought to set this enterprise in motion without delay.

The terrible calamity just narrated did not destroy the courage of this heroic people. Those who were left determined to maintain their plantations. When

Mr. Williams returned to Boston in the flag-ship in 1706, he was met by a committee from Deerfield who invited him to return to his former charge; and though he had received some propositions from a church in the neighborhood of Boston, the brave man went back to the perils of the border, saying, "I must return and look after my sheep in the wilderness." Here he was content to live and labor, and here, after a ministry of forty-three years he was gathered to his rest. A stone in the old burying-ground marks the place where his ashes repose.

During the years that intervened between the destruction of the town in 1704, and the treaty of Utrecht, in 1713, Indian depredations and murders were frequent. Then the land had rest, for a season, and prosperity returned to the homes and the fields of the Deerfield farmers.

Again, in 1744, when many of the heroes of the former conflicts had passed away, war broke out between England and France, and its threatening shadow fell once more upon this peaceful valley. On the 25th of August, 1746, a party of laborers were assailed by the savages at a point in the south meadow known as "The Bars;" several of them were killed and others carried into captivity. Eunice Allen, then a young girl, was pursued by an Indian who plunged his tomahawk into her skull and left her for dead; but she recovered from the frightful wound and lived to be more than eighty years old. This was the last serious collision with the Indians in the history of Deerfield.

Single persons were killed and captured after this time, but nothing occurred which amounted to a disturbance of the tranquillity of the town.

From the hardy men who fought these battles a worthy progeny has sprung, among whom many eminent names are found. Ephraim Williams, Esq., an eminent jurist, and the first reporter of the decisions of the Supreme Court of Massachusetts, was born here, in 1760, married at the age of sixty, and his son —the child of his old age, is the revered and trusted Episcopal bishop of Connecticut. Richard Hildreth, the historian, President Hitchcock of Amherst College, and General Rufus Saxton, all belong by birth to Deerfield. General Epaphras Hoyt, the author of the history upon which liberal drafts have been made in the preparation of this sketch, lived and died in this town. His book is a monument of research, fidelity and literary skill.

Having put ourselves in possession of some of the important facts in the history of this old town we are now prepared to appreciate and enjoy the things we shall see. The road leads southward from the Public Square past the shops of the Russell Manufacturing Company, under the high bridge of the Troy and Greenfield Railroad spanning Green River, through Cheapside, under the bridge of the Connecticut River Railroad, crossing Deerfield River, upon which we looked down from the Bear's Den; across the old wagon bridge, where toll is no longer demanded, and along the eastern border of the Deerfield Meadows.

The owners of two thousand acres of these meadows were for a long time members of a corporation known as "*The Proprietors of the Common Field.*" The fences around the whole were built by the corporation; each man cultivated his own land in the summer, and in the fall, after the crops were gathered, all pastured them in common. The incorporation has lately expired by limitation. Soon we are at the entrance of Deerfield street and it is safe to predict that not many of us have ever seen one more beautiful. It is just a mile in length; and the branches of the majestic elms, meeting over head form a lengthened canopy for the whole of that distance. An old brown house on the right not long after we enter the village is the residence of George Sheldon, Esq.; a gentleman of extensive antiquarian research, and of excellent historical judgment, who has done more than any other living man to collect and sift the traditions of this old town. Mr. Sheldon has one of the largest collections of Indian antiquities to be found in the country. He was the man of whom the witty Springfield *Republican* said that it was his delight to invite a company of antiquarians to supper, and then to amuse them afterward by digging up Indian skulls in his back yard. Mr. Sheldon is now engaged upon a work for which he is thoroughly qualified, and which all his neighbors hope he may live to accomplish—the preparation of a history of his native town. When it is done it will be well done, and no descendant of Deerfield can afford to do without it. The Unitarian Church is a brick edifice on the west side of the street, and at the north end of the Common. The slight elevation on which it stands was known among the early settlers as "Meeting-House Hill." The northern boundary of the old fort ran along this bank; it extended far enough east to enclose the houses on the east side of the street. It was an irregular oblong enclosure, its greatest length being from west to east. The elevation on which it stood was once an island in the lake; and was very likely wooded, when the settlers took possession. A white house stands fronting on the Common directly in the rear of the church, on the spot where the old Indian House stood. The Pocumtuck House is an excellent hotel on the south side of the street, in the hall of which we shall find the Indian Door. The next house beyond the hotel, was probably standing when the town was burnt in 1704. In the Common stands a beautiful shaft of brown freestone, surmounted by the statue of a soldier in fatigue dress, with a rifle at the position of "load." Engraved upon the monument, with various appropriate mottoes, and the names of the battles and prisons in which they gave up their lives are the names of forty-two soldiers,—and this inscription:

"In grateful appreciation of the Patriotism and self-sacrifice of her lamented sons and soldiers, who for their Country and for Freedom laid down their lives in the war of the Great Rebellion, Deerfield erects this monument, A. D. 1867. Their precious dust is scattered on many battle-fields or was hastily buried near some loathsome prison pen; but the memory of their brave deeds and willing sacrifices shall be cherished in our heart of hearts sacredly and forever.

"This Monument stands upon the Old Meeting-House Hill, and is within the limits of the Old Fort, built A. D. 1689, and which remained until A. D. 1758, and was one of the chief defenses of the early settlers against the attacks of savage Indians. With pious affection and gratitude, their descendants would hereby associate the sacrifices and sufferings of the Fathers of the town in establishing our institutions with those of their children in defending them."

"Aye, call it holy ground,
The soil where first they trod
They have left unstained, what here they found,
Freedom to worship God."

The Orthodox Congregational Church is a neat, white edifice on the left hand side of the street, fronting southward. Between the two houses standing north of this church on the principal street, it is said that there was formerly an underground passage provided for the safety of the inmates during the Indian wars. On the south of the common a side street leads down to the old burying-ground, past the old home of President Hitchcock on the left, and the spot on the right where stood the residence of Parson Williams, and where his well still remains. Here lie buried many of the victims of Indian barbarity. The date of th oldest inscription is 1695. A little guide-board marks the spot.

Leaving, now, this quiet street whose atmosphere is pervaded with old memories, let us drive to the top of Pocumtuck Rock, which overlooks the village and the valley. There let us sit down and muse awhile, feasting our eyes upon the beautiful picture at our feet, and supplying in our imagination the scenes that have transpired during the last two hundred years within the circle of these hills.

Another day, perhaps, we will drive further south through the meadows, along the route where Lathrop and his troops and teamsters marched so many years ago, to the spot where they were slaughtered, now marked by a marble cenotaph. This monument was dedicated in 1835, with an oration by Hon. Edward Everett. While we are in this neighborhood too, we will climb to the top of Sugar Loaf, the hill at the base of which the fight took place.

"It is a conical peak of red sandstone, five hundred feet above the plain. It stands on the west bank of the Connecticut, within two hundred yards of the river, and rises almost perpendicularly from the meadows below. Sugar Loaf stands as it were at the head of the valley, and the southern view is remarkable for its beauty. On the left, east of the river, and almost underneath the mountain, is the village of Sunderland, accessible from the west side by a covered bridge. South, and on the same side of the river, are the villages of North Amherst, Amherst, Belchertown, North Hadley and Hadley. On the west side are South Deerfield, Whately, Hatfield, Northampton and Easthampton. Skirting the southern horizon are the lofty peaks of Mounts Holyoke and Tom, and between them, through the gateway to the ocean, glimmering in the sunlight, are the church spires in Holyoke and Chicopee."*

* Burt's Connecticut Valley Guide.

From Greenfield to Sugar Loaf it is only eight miles, —an easy and delightful afternoon excursion; and the ascent of the mountain is not difficult. At the hotel on the summit we may find rest and refreshment.

TURNER'S FALLS.

Up Main street to High street, then northward, along a level and pleasant road. The mills and tenements of the Greenfield Woolen Company stand in Factory Hollow, through which Fall River runs to the Connecticut. A certain eminent actor and elocutionist visiting once at Greenfield rode out this way one fine morning to visit Turner's Falls. On the left hand of the road he saw this mill-dam which he took for the famous cataract,—on the right the frames for drying cloth which he supposed were seats erected for the convenience of visitors to the Falls. Back he galloped to the village and gave free expression to his contempt for people who could make so much fuss about so small a thing. Afterward he went farther and changed his mind. Not far from the mill we catch a glimpse of the Falls through the gorge which Fall River has cloven through the rocks. It is only a glimpse, but it quickens our pulses, and we hurry on to the summit of the hill. And now that this little book may not be charged with too much enthusiasm in its description, let us copy a sketch of the Falls from a work as solid as Hitchcock's Report on the Geology of Massachusetts.

"They are by far the most interesting water-falls in the

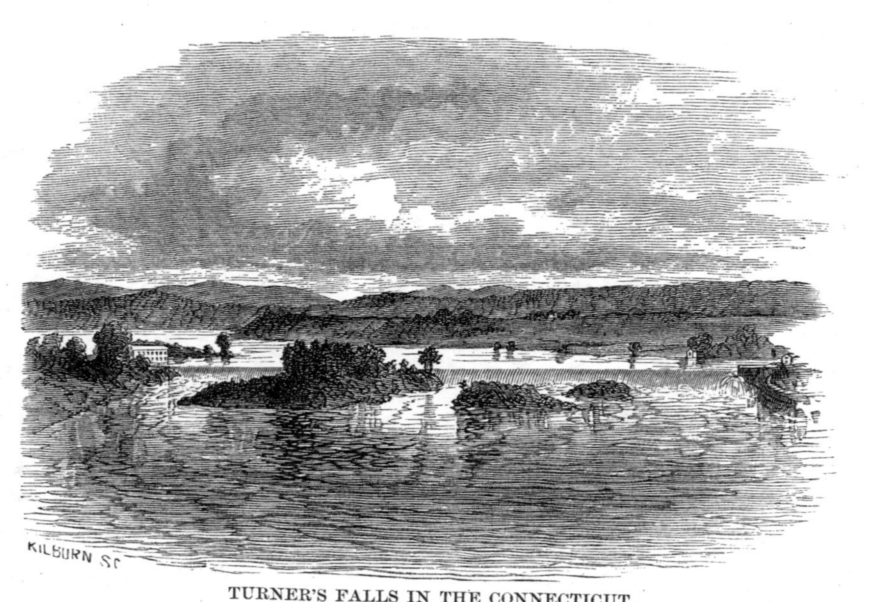

TURNER'S FALLS IN THE CONNECTICUT.

State, and I think I may safely say in New England. Above Turner's Falls the Connecticut for about three miles pursues a course nearly north-west, through a region scarcely yet disturbed by cultivation; and all this distance is as placid as a mountain lake even to the very verge of the cataract. There an artificial dam has been erected, more than a thousand feet long, resting near the center upon two small islands. Over this dam the water leaps more than thirty feet perpendicularly; and for half a mile continues descending rapidly and foaming along its course. One hundred rods below the falls the stream strikes directly against a lofty greenstone ridge, by which it it compelled to change its course towards the south at least a quarter of a mile. The proper point for viewing Turner's Falls is from the road leading to Greenfield on the north shore, perhaps fifty rods below the cataract—[just where we are standing now.] Here from elevated ground you have directly before you the principal fall intersected near the center by two small rocky islands which are crowned by trees and brush-wood. The observer perceives at once that Niagara is before him in miniature. These islands may be reached by a canoe from above the falls with perfect safety. Fifty rods below the cataract a third most romantic little island lifts its evergreen head,—an image of peace and security in the midst of the agitated and foaming waters swiftly gliding by. The placid aspect of the waters above the fall, calmly emerging from the moderately elevated and wooded hills at a distance is finely contrasted with the foam and tumult below the cataract. During high water, the roar of Turner's Falls may be heard from six to ten miles. The magnificence of the cataract is greatly heightened at such a season."

Here occurred the famous Falls Fight. On the evening of the 17th of May, 1676, about eight months after the terrible massacre at Sugar Loaf, Captain Turner marched with one hundred and sixty mounted men from Hatfield, twenty miles below, to attack the Indians who had gathered here to fish in large numbers. Just before daybreak they reached an elevated hill not far from where the woolen mill now stands, where they dismounted, fastened their horses, and crossing Fall River, climbed to the spot where we are standing now, and looked down upon an Indian camp which was pitched near the head of the falls. The Indians were all in a profound sleep without even a watch. "Roused from their slumbers by the sudden roar of musketry they fled, toward the river, vociferating 'Mohawks! Mohawks!' believing this furious enemy was upon them. Many leaped into their canoes, some in the hurry forgetting their paddles and attempting to swim were shot by the English or precipitated down the dreadful cataract and drowned; while others were killed in their cabins or took shelter under the shelving rocks of the river bank, where they were cut down by their assailants without much resistance. The loss of the Indians was severe, one hundred were left dead on the ground, and one hundred and forty were seen to pass down the cataract, but one of whom escaped drowning. A few gained the opposite shore and joined their companions on that side. The whole loss, as was afterwards acknowledged, amounted to above three hundred of all descriptions, among whom were many of their principal sachems."*

Only one Englishman was killed. On his return, however, the Indians, whose force greatly outnumbered Turner's, rallied, and pursued him; dividing and scattering his little army, and killing Turner himself, with thirty-eight of his men.

A short distance above the falls we cross by a ferry from the town of Gill to the town of Montague, and drive down the stream to the new city, whose foundations are now being laid. The dam which Dr. Hitchcock describes is not the one now standing. In 1792 a company was incorporated under the title of the "Proprietors of the Upper Locks and Canals in the County of Hampshire," that built a dam and a canal three miles long at this point, for the purpose of facilitating the navigation of the river. In 1866, the name of this corporation was changed to The Turner's Falls Company, seven hundred acres of land were purchased by them; a new dam was built,—the streets and avenues of a new city were laid out, and one of the largest water powers in New England was developed. This dam is one thousand feet long, in two curved sections; and it has an average fall of thirty-six feet. It is built

*Hoyt's Indian Wars, p. 139.

of timber and entirely filled with stone, making it practically a stone dam. While the dam was building, in the winter of 1866–7, a portion of it about one hundred feet in length was carried away. The whole Connecticut River poured with tremendous force through this opening a hundred feet in width, and the hydraulic engineers declared that the section could not be restored. But a plain man in Greenfield, whose name is George W. Potter, and who is not an engineer, said it could be done, and did it. It was probably one of the most difficult feats of hydraulic engineering ever attempted. Standing on the bulk-head, the view of the fall and the rapids below is magnificent.

Below this dam two canals are being constructed, the one twenty-five feet above the other; and upon these two canals, provision is made for thirty-one mill sites, averaging three hundred horse power each. This does not utilize more than half of the power. The property is rapidly being taken up. The Russell Manufacturing Company are erecting one building six hundred and ten feet long by fifty feet wide; and this is only about one-third of the area of the buildings to be erected by them. Their new shops will give employment to twelve hundred men. Other mills will soon be built, and within twenty years we may expect to see a city of fifteen thousand inhabitants upon this ground.

In the new red sandstone, which constitutes the banks of the river at the Falls, were found the fossil foot-prints which were such a prize to the geologists.

Somewhere from fifty to a hundred thousand years ago, a large number of birds of both sexes and all sizes (some of them standing not less than ten feet without their stockings) were in the habit of walking out at low water on the beach of a lake or estuary, then occupying these parts. Their foot-prints, hardened by the sun, were afterward filled by the rising water with sand and mud; and then the whole mass was petrified. How do we know all this? Look here madam! You must not come round us geologists saying you want to know, you know. We have made some pretty shrewd guesses, and we intend to stand by them.

We drive homeward, along the serene and somewhat slimy banks of the old canal, musing on these foot-marks with the unpronounceable Greek names, all so neatly classified and labeled. Cuvier said that if you would give him a single bone he could construct the skeleton of the animal. But these geologists make pictures of the ancient birds by studying the tracks they left in the primitive mud. Imagine the pictures which will be drawn by geologists fifty or a hundred thousand years hence, when the tracks that were made last summer in the sand at Newport or Long Branch are quarried out of the rock! Imagine a geologist studying the fossil track of a Grecian bender and trying to frame a figure to correspond!

The moral is, ladies, that you should never walk in the mud.

Down through the single street of what was to have

been and still is called a City, whose other name is Montague; across the old bridge which is to give place for a new one for both wagons and cars, where the railroad is to cross now building to Turner's Falls; over the hill, looking backward to take our last leave of the beautiful Connecticut, and down into the village again, by a road that has grown familiar.

OTHER DRIVES.

The Stillwater Drive is deservedly popular about Greenfield. The road to Conway is followed, which leads across the railroad track, then turns to the right, crosses Pettis' Plain, where De Rouville's French and Indians halted on the morning when they made their assault upon Old Deerfield; then turns to the left along the margin of the old lake which is now the meadow, having in sight continually a most beautiful landscape; passes over Stillwater Bridge, into that part of the meadow called "The Bars," where the last fight occurred, and returns by way of Old Deerfield.

Leyden Glen or *Gorge* is a place much visited by tourists. A large brook has worn a passage from ten to twenty feet wide, and from thirty to fifty feet deep in the strata of argillo-micaceous slate. The length of the gorge is about forty rods. Above the gorge is a deep glen, and below it the stream passes through a ravine. Two beautiful water-falls near the mouth of the gorge greatly add to the picturesqueness of the spot. It compares not unfavorably with the famous Flume at the White Mountains. Not far from the entrance to the glen, the place is pointed out where Mrs. Eunice Williams was murdered on the march to Canada.

Romantic and delightful roads pass through *The Shelburne* and *Coleraine Gorges;* you can go by the one and return by the other.

One of the roads to Shelburne takes you for a long distance through cool and pleasant woods, and for three or four miles a brook is your constant companion. Beyond the woods you look back upon another charming view of Greenfield and the Deerfield Valley.

These are only part of the pleasant excursions you can make in the neighborhood of Greenfield. For the rest, consult Stevens of the Mansion House. There are two of them and either of them is a host in more senses than one. What they cannot tell you about things worth seeing in this region is not worth knowing.

CHAPTER III.

FROM GREENFIELD TO NORTH ADAMS.

THE Troy and Greenfield Railroad, from Greenfield to the Hoosac Tunnel, is owned by the Commonwealth of Massachusetts, but is leased and operated by the Vermont and Massachusetts Railroad Company. The airy and pleasant cars of this company take us on board at the Greenfield station, and we are soon passing over the high bridge across Green River, and steaming swiftly along the table-land that overlooks the Deerfield Valley. *West Deerfield* is the name of the station at Stillwater; and just before reaching it we look far away across the meadows upon two peaks in the southern horizon which must be Tom and Holyoke. The gorge from which the Deerfield River emerges, and into which we enter at this point, is the wildest and most beautiful spot we have yet found in our railroading. "As to the defile," says Dr. Hitchcock in his Geological Report, "through which Deerfield River runs between Shelburne and Conway, it is so narrow that it is difficult even on foot to find a passage; though full of romantic and sublime objects to the man who has the strength and courage to pass through it." But what the turnpike did not dare to do the railroad has done; it has hugged the river closely all the way, and thus has given us a constant succession of magnificent scenes, of which the highway altogether defrauded the traveler. Any elaborate description of these scenes is superfluous. The traveler must not be looking in his book; he must be looking out of the window.

Shelburne Falls is a thriving town twelve miles from Greenfield. The cataract in the Deerfield at this point is a beautiful one, though the glimpse of it that we get from the cars is hardly satisfactory. Here is another mammoth cutlery establishment, next to the Russell Works at Greenfield in size and importance. Messrs. Lamson and Goodnow are the proprietors. The excellent water-power afforded by these falls is turned to good account in manufacturing. Here resided, until his death within the past year, Mr. Linus Yale, Jr., whose father picked the locks of Hobbes, the Englishman, so cleverly, and who himself made a lock that the Englishman could not pick. The Yale locks, known everywhere, are made here. The village of Shelburne Falls puts in a fine appearance, scattered along the narrow valley, and upon the adjacent hill-sides. Two churches confronting each other on one of the streets made us think of Dr. Holmes, who, you know, was always reminded, when he saw two churches situated in this manner, of a pair of belligerent roosters, with tails erect and crests ruffled, eyeing each other at close quarters. These two churches, it is pleasant to know, are not in a state of war, nor even in a condition of armed neutrality, though their edifices may be in a threatening attitude.

Beyond Shelburne Falls is *Buckland*, a small station where travelers will be amused to see a sort of telegraphic contrivance for carrying the mail across the river. It is a good illustration of Yankee ingenuity. Part of the territory of Buckland was formerly called "No Town." To this unpretending old town, the thoughts of many will make pilgrimages, though their eyes may never see the glory of its wooded hills. It was the birthplace of Mary Lyon. Here the valley of the Deerfield, which for much of the distance since we left Stillwater has been only a gorge, grows a little wider, and there are good farms, with excellent orchards, on both sides of the river. Without doubt, this valley, in which part of Buckland and nearly the whole of Charlemont lie, was once a lake. But though the hills recede from the river they do not lose their attractiveness. Their symmetrical outlines present to us a constant and charming variety of graceful and beautiful forms. This river, whose banks we follow,—now lying placidly in the midst of green meadows, or winding through willow thickets; now rippling with a musical delight, which we can feel if we cannot hear it, over broad and shallow places; now reflecting in its smooth pure waters, long reaches of shingly shores or islands; now plunging madly down tortuous rapids;

this matchless Deerfield River is to every traveler who follows its course a ceaseless fascination, a perpetual delight. The quickest and most loving eye seizes but few of its many charms in one journey; and with as poor a pigment as printers' ink one could hardly paint them.

Charlemont is an old town, extending fourteen miles along the river; and from one to three miles wide. The principal village is across the river from the railroad, and among other distinguishments boasts one of the best old fashioned country inns to be found anywhere this side the water. "Deacon" Dalrymple, the inn-keeper, is a character in his way. The figure of speech by which his title is applied to him is not down in the historical books; but his inn, unlike his title, is not a figure of speech at all. If you want a good, square, country meal, with no nonsense about it, the Deacon is your man. And yet, so indifferent is he to patronage and so averse to praise, that he will be likely to resent this little notice as a mortal injury; and the writer will never dare to show himself on that side of the river. The only motive of this paragraph is the public good. There are so few good country taverns in the land that any man in such a place who can keep a hotel, and wont keep a hotel ought to be made to keep a hotel.

The old town has sent forth some celebrities. Ex-Governor Washburne was born here; Rev. Roswell Hawkes, and Rev. Theron M. Hawkes, both well known Orthodox ministers are natives of this town;

Hon. Joseph White, Secretary of the Board of Education, hails from this valley.

In early days this town included a part of what is now Heath, the town adjoining it on the north. During the Revolution, Rev. Jonathan Leavitt, father of Hon. Jonathan Leavitt, of the Court of Common Pleas, and of Dr. Joshua Leavitt of the New York *Independent*, was the Congregational pastor here, and made no small stir among his people in one way and another. He was not quite sound in his theology, many thought; he was not so ardent a Whig as some of his townsmen, and his views on the subject of finance troubled them exceedingly. It seems that the town (the town and the parish were identical in those days) had voted before the war to give him so much salary; and when the Continental paper money had depreciated so that it wasn't worth a Continental, they wanted to pay the parson in that, to which he strenuously objected. When they cast him out of the church, he entered into the school-house and preached there; and after the war he sued the towns of Heath and Charlemont for the arrearages in his salary. The lower court decided against him, but the Supreme Court reversed the decision, and awarded to Mr. Leavitt £500 for preaching in the school-house, and £200 for loss suffered through the depreciation of paper currency. If all the dominies in the land should collect by law from their parishes the difference in their salaries between gold and greenbacks during the late war, some of them would have money enough to take a trip to Europe.

In this quarrel between Mr. Leavitt and his parish, no doubt the parson had the law on his side; but the methods he took of enforcing his claims are open to severe criticism. As much might be said of some of his antagonists. It is the theory of the Congregational order that one church may not interfere with the affairs of another except to give advice when it is called for; but in this quarrel we find Rev. Mr. Jones, of Rowe, coming uninvited at the head of a posse of his parishioners, to give advice to Mr. Leavitt, and bearing in his hand not exactly an olive branch, or the emblematical balances, but a bayonet fastened to the end of a rake's-tail! Advice, under most circumstances is easier to prescribe than to swallow; but under such circumstances it would certainly be classed among those commodities which it is more blessed to give than to receive. It does not appear that Mr. Leavitt was persuaded by these urgent solicitations of his brethren.

Above Charlemont the scenery grows wilder. Now we are plunging into the heart of this beautiful region. The valley contracts to a narrow gorge; the hills, wooded from base to summit, rise abruptly from the river-bed a thousand feet into the air. How the river finds its passage among them we cannot always make out. Looking before us, we can discover no break in the solid chain of hills; looking behind us the mountain wall is equally impenetrable. Still the river has leisure. Doubtless it can make its way. Rivers always do. But how are these thundering, screaming cars to thrid this Titan's Labyrinth? Is there not danger that they will come to a sudden halt against that solid mountain at which they are driving so furiously? The danger always passes before we have had time to be alarmed. The cul-de-sac has always an opening. The train skips across the river, bends sharply round a curve, and darts with a yell of triumph into a new defile. It is a Titan's Labyrinth, but the strength and swiftness and cunning that are searching out and forcing open its hidden paths for us are more than Titanic.

Next above Charlemont the train halts at *Zoar*. "Is it not a little one?" said the patriarch Lot of the city of that name to which he fled. Certainly this is not a very big one. It might be large enough to hold a patriarch, but there certainly is not room for a lot in it,—for a level one at any rate. Somebody at your elbow who knows more than he ought to know suggests that Lot was not always exactly level!

Beyond Zoar the grandeur grows apace. We pass on the left a covered bridge under which a cataract tumbles; the hills are closer, higher, and steeper; the foliage on their sides more dense and richer in variety. Soon a little green valley laughs at us from across the river; the train slackens its speed, the brakeman shouts "*Hoosac Tunnel!*" and we gather our bundles and disembark.

Dinner at Rice's, an old and excellent country tavern

DEERFIELD RIVER AT THE EASTERN PORTAL.

across the river; and then, perhaps we will spend the afternoon in exploring this region, and in making ourselves familiar with what is here to be seen of

THE HOOSAC TUNNEL.

Up to this point the Deerfield River has given us an excellent route for a railroad. But just here we find it coming down from the north, out of the fastnesses of the Green Mountains. It would not be easy to follow its course any higher; and it would lead us where we do not wish to go. Right across the westward path which we have followed nature has written, in the bold horizon lines of the Hoosac Mountain, "No Thoroughfare." But many of Nature's legends get rubbed out and this one soon will be.

The project of tunneling this mountain is not a new one. In 1825 a board of commissioners with Loami Baldwin as engineer, were appointed by the Legislature to ascertain the practicability of making a canal from Boston to the Hudson River. They examined the country by way of Worcester, Springfield, and the Westfield River; and also by Fitchburg, and the Miller and Deerfield Rivers, making the village of North Adams a point common to both routes; and reported that "there was no hesitation in deciding in favor of the Deerfield and Hoosac River Route."

At the Hoosac their examinations were extended both to the north and south of the present line of tunnel with a view to discover some other route by which it might be avoided, but increased distance and lackage and difficulty of procuring water led them to give preference to the tunnel. In their report they say: "There is no hesitation, therefore, in deciding in favor of a tunnel; but even if its expense should exceed the other mode of passing the mountain, a tunnel is preferable, for the reasons which have been assigned. And this formidable barrier once overcome, the remainder of the route, from the Connecticut to the Hudson presents no unusual difficulties in the construction of a canal, but in fact the reverse; being remarkably feasible."

During this very year, the first railway was opened in America for the conveyance of freight and passengers, and the attention of the people being turned to this improved method of communication the project of building a canal from Boston to Troy was abandoned. The Boston and Albany Railroad was completed in 1842, but the advantages of this northern route were never lost sight of. The thriving towns along the line looked for an outlet east and west, and the vast undeveloped resources of the region through which the railroad would pass gave abundant encouragement to the prosecution of the work. In 1845 the first section of the road was opened to Fitchburg; shortly afterward the Vermont and Massachusetts Railroad was begun; and as early as 1848 the Troy and Greenfield Railroad Company was incorporated by the Legislature, with a capital of three million five hundred thousand dollars, and was authorized to build a railroad "from the terminus of the Vermont and Massachusetts Railroad at Greenfield, through the valleys of the Deerfield and Hoosac to the State line, there to unite with a railroad leading to the city of Troy." The road must be located within two years, and finished within seven years.

The feasibility of the undertaking was not apparent to capitalists, however; and at the end of six years the subscription books of the company showed a beggarly array of blank pages, while almost nothing had been done towards the construction of the road. Efforts had been made during this time to obtain a State loan; but it was not till 1854 that the Commonwealth loaned its credit to the company to the amount of two millions of dollars. Under this act a contract was made with E. W. Serrell & Company, and work was begun in earnest in 1855. The conditions under which the loan was granted were found difficult of fulfillment; and the progress of the work was impeded. In 1856 a new contract was made with H. Haupt & Company by which the company agreed to pay three million eight hundred and eighty thousand dollars for completing the road and tunnel. From this time till 1861 the work was carried on by the company and the contractors. Excavations were made at each end of the tunnel, and in 1858 the western section of the road was completed to the State line, connecting North Adams with Troy. In 1861, a difficulty arose between Haupt & Company and the State Engineer concerning the payment of the installments of the State loan, which resulted in the abandonment of the work by the contractors. Nothing farther was done until the winter of 1862, when an act was passed providing that the State should take possession of the road, the tunnel, and all the property of the Troy and Greenfield Company; and appointing a Commission to examine the works and report to the next Legislature. This Commission made an elaborate report in February, 1863, recommending the prosecution of the work by the State; upon which in the autumn of the same year work was resumed by the commissioners, under the able superintendence of Mr. Thomas Doane who had been appointed Chief Engineer. The enterprise was prosecuted by the commissioners until the winter of 1868, when the Legislature made an appropriation of four million seven hundred and fifty thousand dollars for the completion of the work, requiring that it should be contracted by the first of January following. The contract was taken by Messrs. F. Shanly & Brother of Canada, who agree to finish the tunnel and lay the track by March 1, 1874. These gentlemen are now rapidly and vigorously carrying on the work.

The length of the tunnel from portal to portal is a little more than four miles and three quarters, and the rock through which it passes, except at the extreme western end where a secondary formation overlays the primary, is a solid mica slate, with occasional nodules of quartz. The mountain has two crests, with a valley between them. The one which overlooks the Deerfield is about fourteen hundred and fifty feet above the river bed; the one which overlooks the Hoosac is seventeen hundred and fifty feet above the bed of that river. The lowest spot in the depression between these peaks on the line of the tunnel is about eight hundred feet above the grade.

The work is being driven from both ends; and in the valley at the top of the mountain a shaft is being sunk, from which, when the grade is reached, excavations will be pushed, east and west, to meet those that are being driven inward. This shaft besides giving two more faces on which to work, and thus expediting the completion of the tunnel, is expected to afford ventilation when the tunnel is completed.

At first the work was all done by hand-drills; but attempts were soon made to construct machines for rock-cutting. In 1851 a monster of this sort weighing seventy tons was constructed at South Boston, and "was designed to cut out a groove around the circumference of the tunnel, thirteen inches wide and twenty-four feet in diameter, by means of a set of revolving cutters. When this groove had been cut to a proper depth, the machine was to be run back on its railway and the center core blasted out by gunpowder or split off by means of wedges. It was conveyed to the Hoosac mountain, and, the approach not being then completed, was put in operation on a vertical face of rock near the proposed entrance to the tunnel." The Railroad Committee of the Legislature after examining its operations were fully convinced that it was a stupendous success. It was operated under their eyes for full fifteen minutes, during which time it cut into the rock four and one-eighth inches, or at the rate of sixteen and one half inches per hour. At that rate, by operating at both ends, the tunnel could be built in about two years. This was rosy. But unfortunately this mechanical behemoth refused to go on. Ten feet was the extent of its progress. It amounted to old iron and that was all. Nothing daunted by this failure, Mr. Haupt, at an expense of twenty-five thousand dollars, procured another boring machine. This was to excavate the heading only, or a hole eight feet in diameter; which was afterwards to be enlarged by manual labor and blasting. Mr. Haupt was sanguine about this. In a letter to General Wool, under date of September 25, 1858, he prophesies:—"The slowest progress of the machine when working will be fifteen inches per hour; the fastest, twenty-four inches. A machine at each end working but half the time with the slowest speed, should go through the mountain in twenty-six months." But this promising contrivance never made an inch of progress into the rock. It was "an auger that wouldn't bore."

These costly experiments with tunneling machines sufficed. After this the work was done with elbow grease and gunpowder until Mr. Doane took charge of the tunnel, when preparations were immediately made to introduce power drills. These had been successfully employed on the great Mount Cenis Tunnel now constructing under the Alps between France and Sardinia. The impossibility of operating machinery with steam in a tunnel, owing to the fouling of the air with smoke, made it necessary to find some other motive power for the drills; and the engineers of the Mount Cenis Tunnel at length succeeded in solving this problem. Their method with variations and improvements was adopted here. Air compressed by machinery to a pressure of six atmospheres or ninety pounds to the square inch is carried into the tunnel in iron pipes, and there being ejected with the force due to its pressure, it not only serves to move the piston of the machine drill, but ventilates the tunnel. The dam in the Deerfield River just above the eastern portal of the tunnel furnishes the power by which the air-compressors are driven.

Under the management of Mr. Haupt, about two thousand four hundred feet of linear excavation was made at this eastern end. The distance penetrated from the eastern portal at the transfer of the work to the Messrs. Shanly was five thousand two hundred and eighty-two feet—just two feet more than a mile.

THE WEST END.

At the west end the difficulties of the work have been greatest. On this side the mountain wall is less abrupt than on the other; and on entering the slope of the mountain the workmen came upon a solid limestone rock easy of excavation. But this rock soon began to dip, and at length as they progressed, it disappeared below the grade of the tunnel, and they discovered that they had passed through the limestone into what geology calls disintegrated mica and talc schist; but what history with a truer nomenclature, designates as porridge. This loose rock, readily yielding to the action of water and dissolving into a fluid of about the consistency of gruel was a most formidable foe to the engineers. From before its face they retreated, resolving to make an open cutting instead of a tunnel for the first few hundred feet. Accordingly they ascended to the surface, sunk a shaft just eastward of the end of their completed tunnel, and began to take out the earth. But the open cutting was a job of some magnitude. When they had made an immense hopper, five hundred and fifty feet long, three hundred feet wide and seventy-five feet deep, they concluded to try tunneling again. As fast as excavations were made into this demoralized rock it was necessary to make a complete casing of timber to support the sides and roof of the tunnel. Within this casing an arch of masonry must be built. There was no solid foundation on which to rear the walls and roof of masonry; and it was therefore necessary to lay an inverted arch of brick for a flooring. The top of the tunnel is a semicircle, whose radius is thirteen feet; and the sides as well as the invert are arcs of a circle whose radius is twenty-six feet. The invert was carried in for eight hundred and eighty-three feet from the portal; at which point rock was found of sufficient firmness to sustain the walls of masonry. It will be seen therefore that nearly nine hundred feet of the west end is a complete tube of brick, averaging about eight courses in thickness.

Most of this difficult work at the west end was done by Mr. B. N. Farren under a contract with the commissioners. The obstacles have at some times been appalling. So treacherous was the quicksand, and so great the flow of water at times, that whole months have been spent in the most energetic labor without making an inch of progress. It was necessary thoroughly to drain the porridge by side and cross drifts in every direction before anything could be done. For this purpose about twelve hundred feet of extra heading was made outside of the tunnel. When at last they pierced the thin quartz vein which separated the porridge from the mountain rocks, there was great joy in those diggings. Beyond this the rock was soft, but not affected by the action of water; and the troubles of the engineers were at an end.

This demoralized rock, which has given so much grief to the friends of the tunnel has given equal joy to its foes. This has been their constant argument to prove that the tunnel was a blunder and a failure and a swindle. Driven from every other stronghold they have entrenched themselves in this porridge with desperate resolution. Marshalled by the amiable but indomitable Mr. Bird of Walpole, the pamphleteers have let fly at this soft rock a broadside of paper missiles. There are a good many bird-tracks in the new red sandstone at Gill; but the Bird tracts about this porridge are much more numerous.

While part of the miners were fighting with the porridge at the west end, another army of them ascended the mountain side to a point on the line of the tunnel about half a mile east of the west portal, and there sunk a shaft in the solid rock, three hundred and eighteen feet. From this shaft an opening has now been made to the west end, and the heading has been pushed eastward sixteen hundred feet,—making a continuous lineal excavation of four thousand fifty-six feet from the west portal to the end of the heading.

The cost of this work is not an insignificant item. Up to the time when the commissioners took possession of the road the State had advanced nearly a million of dollars. The commissioners have expended \$3,229,530. The Messrs. Shanly are to receive for completing the work, \$4,594,268. Add to these sums the amount required to finish the road from the tunnel to North Adams, and the total cost of the road and the tunnel according to the last estimate of the commissioners will be a little over nine millions of dollars.

If anybody wants to know what advantages are to be derived from this large expenditure, the answers are easy. This road will shorten the distance from Boston to Troy by nine miles; and on account of its easier gradients, will be a much better road for freights than the Western. It will thus give greatly increased facilities for trade between Boston and the West, and will by its competition reduce the enormous prices of transportation over the Boston and Albany Road. At the same time it will help to develop the resources of the country through which it passes, and will open to pleasure as well as to business a most attractive and profitable line of travel.

The longest tunnel now in use is the Woodhead Tunnel on the Manchester, Sheffield and Lincolnshire Railroad,—a short distance from Manchester, England. This is a little more than three miles long. The Nerthe Tunnel in France, between Marseilles and Avignon is nearly as long. The great tunnel before referred to, now constructing under the Alps at Mount Cenis, is more than seven miles and a half in length. The Hoosac will therefore, when it is constructed, be the longest tunnel in the world with the exception of the one at Mount Cenis.

Now if the ladies will array themselves in their shortest skirts, their oldest hats, their water-proofs, and their over-shoes, we will go forth and see what we have been reading about. From Rice's to the tunnel the road runs along the river side, part of the way under a delightful canopy of forest trees, and part of the way upon a precipitous bank. In the bend of the river lies the immense pile of rock removed from the tunnel. Passing by the stores, and crossing the track that issues from the portal we follow the stream up to the Deerfield Dam, a structure built for use, and answering its purpose well; but like all the best works of man, as beautiful as it is useful. Retracing our steps we descend the stream to the machine-shops and compressor building, in which we watch for a few moments the slow but mighty movement of the enormous air pumps which supply the motive power to the drills that are hammering away upon the face of the rock more than a mile distant in the heading of the tunnel. Here too we may see one of the drilling-machines brought in for repairs. It is the invention of Mr. Charles Burleigh of Fitchburg; and it consists of a cylinder and piston operated by the elastic force of compressed air. The drill is fastened to the piston, and is driven into the rock by repeated strokes of the piston.

To the left of the track as we approach the portal we can see the hole in the rock made by the big borer some years ago. A little tool-shop occupies the niche. Perhaps we shall have time before we go in to ascend this brook which flows past the mouth of the tunnel, for a quarter of a mile to the Cascade of the Twins. Two rivulets that unite to form this brook, coming from different directions, tumble over the rocks from a height of fifty or sixty feet into the same little pool. It is a good place to spend an hour or two upon a hot day.

On our return the train is in readiness. "All aboard!" shouts the conductor, who is also the engineer, likewise the brakeman. He is dressed in an over-coat of dirty yellow rubber cloth; and he flourishes a rawhide. The cars upon which we mount are not exactly drawing-room cars, but they answer tolerably well. The locomotive is a good sized mule, who lowers his long ears, bends his strong back, and makes for the portal. In we go! The blue canopy over head gives place to the dripping rock, a breeze

HOOSAC TUNNEL.—EASTERN PORTAL.

coming out of the mountain and produced by the air escaping from the drills at the distant heading greets us; and we soon perceive that we have passed out of the summer heat into a much cooler temperature. Perhaps, too, if there has been a recent blast we shall meet odors and vapors coming forth from this darkness which will remind us of Tartarus, rather than of the Cave of the winds. By and by an unearthly clangor reaches our ears; in the murky distance lurid lights and goblin shapes are seen flitting and stalking about; and presently we are in the very workshop of Vulcan himself; in the midst of noises dire and forms uncouth, and faces grimy and hideous. The drilling-machines are fastened to a massive iron frame which is pushed up against the face of the rocks; when holes enough are perforated, the frame is pushed back; little tin cartridges of nitro-glycerine to each of which the wires of a galvanic battery is attached, are placed in the holes; the workmen retire to safe distances; the galvanic circuit is completed, and a sound like all the noises of an earthquake and a thunder-storm rolled into one, followed by a tremendous rush of air toward the portal, announces that a few more inches of the Hoosac Tunnel are completed.

A very short visit to this interesting spot generally satisfies nervous people; wherefore we will speedily remount our conveyance and turn our faces toward daylight.

When the heats of noon are past, and the sun begins to sink behind the Hoosac Mountain we will prepare for our stage ride of eight miles to North Adams. There is a vulgar prejudice against that excellent and time-honored institution called the stage-coach, but this prejudice is rarely able to survive the journey over the Hoosac Mountain. Persons who have made this overland trip have discovered that the true luxury and glory of travel are only to be found in the stage-coaches. Fatigued with the journey in the cars to this point they have alighted from the stages on the other side refreshed and vigorous. The change from the cars to the stages is always restful. The grand scenery and the bracing air of the mountain are full of delicious intoxication. If mere bodily comfort were sought in travel the stage ride could not well be omitted; but they who seek refreshment for their minds will readily allow that these eight miles over the Hoosac Mountain are worth more than all the rest of the journey. The only objection to the tunnel worthy of a moment's consideration is that it will deprive many travelers of this precious interlude.

Under the lengthening shadows our train of elegant six-horse coaches begin to climb the mountain. Barnes & Co. are the names written over the coach doors. Barnes is the popular host of the United States Hotel at Boston, and " Co." includes " Jim Stevens," one of our drivers, who with " Al Richardson," another of the drivers, manages the business here. " Jim " was once somebody's baby, but that must have been some time ago. It wouldn't be much of a pastime to dandle him now. It is pleasant to know that his skill and trustworthiness as a stage-driver are in direct proportion to his size. He might, perhaps, be bigger than he is; he could not possibly be a better driver. To sit by his side and see him handle the reins on one of these mountain trips, deftly turning his long team round the sharp angles in the steep road; quietly making every horse do his part on the heavy up hill stretches, and coolly keeping them all in hand in the crooked descent, and all without swearing or shouting or whipping, is to enjoy one of the triumphs of horsemanship. "Jim" learned his trade in a long apprenticeship among the White Hills, and he is fond of talking about that region; and yet he maintains that the scenery of this stage ride over the Hoosac is hardly surpassed in that famous resort of travelers. It ought to be conceded that the opinions of men like "Jim" and "Al," whose avoirdupois balances are respectively three hundred and twenty and two hundred and thirty pounds, are entitled to some weight.

Steady climbing now for forty minutes. The road creeps cautiously up the mountain side,—much of the way through the forest, but often revealing the rugged grandeur of the hills. Now you begin to get some adequate idea of the depth and sinuosity of this Deerfield Gorge. Half a mile from Rice's is Puck's Nook, where the road makes a sharp turn to the north, crossing one of the Twin Rivulets, which here comes gurgling out of a dense thicket above the road, and leaps merrily down a steep ravine upon our right. A little farther on, we emerge from the woods, and climbing a steep pitch, look down into the valley out of which we have ascended. The green meadows, the orchards, the river, the bridge, the shady road along the bank, the neat white hostelry of Jenks & Rice, and the other buildings nested in this snug little valley, and around them all, built up into the sky, the steep, solid battlement of hills! It would not do to call this valley a basin; the bottom is too small, and the sides are too high and steep; it is a cup rather,—the drinking cup of a Titan—embossed as the seasons pass with green and gold and garnet forests, and drained of all but a few sparkling drops of the crystal flood with which it once was overbrimming.

On the hill across the river the line of the tunnel is marked by a narrow path cut through the forest to a signal station on the top. A white object upon that hill-top furnishes a perpetual conundrum to travelers: the guesses are commonly divided between a white cow, a pale horse and a shanty. It may give relief to some minds to know that it is a rock. When you are exactly in the range of that line on the opposite hill you are exactly over the tunnel; and you will notice similar paths cut through the forests both above and below the road. "Jim" says that one lady on being told that the stage was at that moment passing over the tunnel, ejaculated with a little scream, "Oh! I thought it sounded hollow!"

A long pull and a strong pull of Jim's honest blacks and grays brings us to the top of the eastern crest of the Hoosac Mountain. Now look! You have but a few moments,—make the most of them. You may travel far but you will never look upon a fairer scene than that. The vision reaches away for miles and miles over the tops of a hundred hills grouped in beautiful disorder. Fifty miles as the crow flies from the spot where you are standing, the cone of old Monadnock pierces the sky. Further south, and ten miles farther away, the top of Wachusett is seen in a clear day dimly outlined in the horizon. Down at your feet flows the deep gorge of the Deerfield whose course you can trace for many miles. Nothing is seen at first view but these rugged hills and the deep ravines that divide them—no trace or token of meadow or lowland; but some subtile enchantment presently attracts the eye to that miniature valley out of which we have climbed, bordered on one side by the Deerfield, and walled in on all the other sides by the steepest hills. This little valley at once becomes the center of the picture; from it the eye makes many wide excursions over the hill-tops but it hastens back again. It is like a ballad in the middle of a symphony; the symphony is grand, but the ballad keeps singing itself over in your memory at every pause. And yet that is a very tame little valley, or would be anywhere else. Its smooth, green fields edged by the river, would never attract a glance in any level country. But, shut in here, as it is among these hills,—the only sign of quiet amid all these tokens of universal force,—it is unspeakably beautiful. The mountains, too, are grander and wilder by the contrast with this peaceful scene. Every artist, whether in words or colors ought to look upon this landscape. It would teach him a useful lesson.

Over the crest of the mountain, westward, swiftly down into the valley of the Cold River, which divides the eastern from the western summit. The stunted beeches on the left, barren of branches on the north-west side, show how fierce the winter winds are, and from what quarter they come. This summit is two thousand one hundred and ten feet above tide water, and the western summit is four hundred feet higher. Over the top of the hill in the west we catch our first glimpse of Greylock.

Beyond the lowest part of the valley, on the slope of the western crest, the new buildings over the Central Shaft of the tunnel are seen. At this place, on the 19th of October, 1867, a horrible casualty took place. Thirteen men were at work at the bottom of the shaft, five hundred and eighty-three feet from the surface, when the accidental explosion of a tank of gasoline which had been used in lighting the shaft suddenly set the buildings over the shaft into a blaze. The engineer was driven from his post, the hoisting apparatus was disabled and inaccessible, and the terrible certainty was at once forced upon the minds of all who looked on, that the men at the bottom of the shaft were doomed. How soon or in what manner the men were themselves made aware of their awful condition or in what way they met their fate no one will ever know. Some doubtless were killed by the

CENTRAL SHAFT.—MALLORY'S PERILOUS DESCENT.

falling timbers of the building; and by a terrible hail of steel drills precipitated into the shaft when the platform gave way; others, perhaps, were suffocated by the bad air, and others possibly were drowned by the rising water, after the pumps stopped working. The next morning, as soon as the smoking ruins could be cleared away, a brave miner named Mallory was lowered by a rope around his body to the bottom of the shaft, and found there ten or fifteen feet of water on the top of which were floating blackened timbers and debris from the ruins, but saw no traces of the men. It was impossible even to rescue their bodies. The water was rapidly filling up the shaft, and new buildings must be erected and proper machinery procured before it could be removed. It was not till the last days of October, 1868, a full year after the accident, that the bottom of the shaft was reached and the bodies were secured.

On this bleak, rough mountain top, lies all that is inhabitable of the town of Florida. There are a few good grazing farms, but grain has a slim chance between the late and early frosts. The winters are long and fierce. During the Revolutionary War a body of troops attempted to make the passage of this mountain in midwinter, and nearly perished with cold and hunger. Jim can tell you some large stories, if he chooses, about the storms and drifts of last winter. Passing on the left a dilapidated old tavern, where none but a stranger will be likely to get taken in, and on the right, as we ascend the western crest, a smooth surface of rock with furrows chiseled in it by primitive icebergs, there suddenly bursts upon us a scene whose splendor makes abundant compensation for the dreariness of the last three miles.

In the center of the picture rises Greylock, King of Mountains; about him are the group of lesser peaks that make his court. On the north, Mount Adams, a spur of the Green Mountain range, closes the scene. Between this and the Greylock group the beautiful curves of the Taghkanic range fill the western horizon. From the north flows down, through the valley that separates the mountain on which we stand from Mount Adams, the north branch of the Hoosac river; from the south, through the village of South Adams and the valley that lies between us and Greylock, comes the other branch of the river; right at our feet and fifteen hundred feet below us lies the village of North Adams, packed in among its ravines and climbing the slopes on every side; and here the two branches of the Hoosac unite and flow on westward through the other valley that divides Greylock from Mount Adams. Williamstown lies at the foot of the Taconic Hills, just behind the spur of Mount Adams. The straight line of the Pittsfield and North Adams Railroad cuts the southern valley in twain; the Troy and Boston railroad bisects the western valley; and the twin spires of little Stamford in Vermont brighten the valley on the north. These three deep valleys, with the village at their point of confluence, and the lordly mountain walls that shut them in, give us a picture whose beauty will not be eclipsed by any scene that New England can show us. If it should fall to your lot, good reader, as it fell to the lot of one (whether in the body or out of the body I cannot tell) to stand upon the rock that overhangs the road by which we are descending, while the sun, hiding behind amber clouds in the west, touches the western slopes of the old mountain there in the center with the most delicate pink and purple hues,—while the shadows gather in the hollows of its eastern side,—and the sweet breath of a summer evening steals over the green meadows where the little river winds among its alder bushes,—if this should be your felicity, you will say, and reverently too: "It is good to be here; let us make tabernacles and abide; for surely there shall never rest upon our souls a purer benediction!"

People often debate whether this view from the western crest be not finer than that from the eastern; but with many the preference always rests with that which they have looked on last.

Down the steep zigzags we go steadily, round the hills and through the gorges we wind merrily, past the mills and tenements of the upper village we clatter briskly, and soon the stages halt before the imposing front of the Wilson House; in which, unless we prefer the less spacious but comfortable Berkshire House across the way, we shall find quarters, if we are wise, for more than one night.

CHAPTER IV.

UNDER THE SHADOW OF GREYLOCK.

NO one can say of this town of Adams, what the member from Essex spitefully said of one of the towns through which we have passed,—that it is like a growing potato—the best part of it under ground. Adams has not buried many of its heroes,—partly because it has not had many to bury, and partly because it is a theory widely accepted in the town that the worst use to which talent can be put is to bury it. The town was born amid the throes of the Revolution; being incorporated in 1776, and taking its name from the famous Sam Adams. The first settlers were from Connecticut; most of these died or removed, and their lands fell into the possession of emigrants from Rhode Island, many of whom were Quakers. The southern part of the town is now largely populated by the descendants of this peaceful sect; one at least of whom has made herself a national reputation. The clear-minded, large-minded, and by no means weak-minded Susan B. Anthony was born under the shadow of Greylock. Some of the first families of Adams can trace the lines of their ancestry up to the Pilgrims who came over with Bradford and Standish in the Mayflower; the rest are all descendants of the original passengers, who came over with Noah in the ark. The ordinary sort of aristocracy does not, therefore, prevail in Adams to any alarming extent. There is wealth here,—but all of it has been earned; none of it was inherited. All the leading business men began life with no stock in trade but brains and courage. Out of this capital they have created fortunes for themselves, and have built up a flourishing town. The population of the town has increased with great rapidity during the last few years, and the appreciation of property and the increase of business have kept even pace with the growth of population. The value of goods manufactured in 1868, which was a dull year for business, is shown by the books of the Internal Revenue Department to be above seven millions of dollars. That is not an exaggerated statement at any rate. The town contains two calico printing establishments, twelve cotton mills, eight woolen mills, four shoe factories, one tannery, two carriage manufactories, three paper mills, two flouring mills, two sash and blind factories, and two machine shops. In these not less than thirty-five hundred operatives and mechanics find employment, and the wages paid by manufacturers to their employes amount to more than a million and a quarter of dollars.

These statistics include both the north and the south

villages of Adams; North Adams having rather more than two-thirds of the population and the business.

It does not take the traveler long to discover that North Adams is a village of great vigor and enterprise. Capital is not suffered to lie idle in the vaults of banks; it is constantly in motion. It is a thoroughly democratic town. The factitious class distinctions so commonly observed in the society of our larger villages are not very obvious here. There is a more thorough fusion of the various social orders than is usually found. At a reception in the spacious parlors of one of the wealthy citizens you will meet people of widely different stations and conditions, all on a footing of social equality. The morality of the town is considerably above the average of villages of its class. Manufacturing communities as large as this are always far from perfect; but in a town that votes as this one did last year, in a hotly contested struggle, three to one against the licensing of open bars for the sale of liquor, drunkenness cannot be a very general vice; and it is fair to estimate the morality of the town in other respects by its vote on this question. It is quite common, in certain quarters, for various reasons, to disparage the town of Adams, but readers of this little book will discover after stopping a week at the Wilson House that there are many worse places.

A few elegant houses recently erected, three new churches, and a magnificent new school-house on the hill, in the centre of the village, which cost eighty thousand dollars, show that the attention of the people is being turned to architectural improvements. The Wilson House is quite a phenomenon in a village of this size, and visitors may be interested to know who built it, and how it happened to be built.

This hotel is the property of Mr. Allen B. Wilson, the inventor of the Wheeler and Wilson Sewing Machine, now a resident of Waterbury, Conn. The story of his life, though wanting in tragic situations and remarkable feats, is worth reading. It is the same old story of struggle and want and ultimate triumph which has been told of so many American inventors.

Wilson was born in the town of Willett, Cortland County, N. Y. His father died in his early childhood, and at the age of fifteen he was bound out to a relative to learn the triple trade of carpenter, joiner and cabinet maker. This trade was supposed by his employer to include such work as mowing Canada thistles, milking cows and making maple sugar, at which Wilson was kept the greater part of the time. Not fancying these branches of the business, the apprentice ran away after two years to a safe place among the Catskill Mountains, where he hired out as a cabinet-maker. In 1847 he started westward as a tramping journeyman, in search of a fortune, working at cabinet-making and carving in Cleveland, Chicago and several other Western towns. At Burlington he was attacked and prostrated by the fever and ague, a disease that followed him for seven years, and nearly wrecked him. Slowly and sadly he made his way back to his country home in Cortland County, where he passed a miserable winter, very poor in purse, and nearly broken in spirit. In the spring of '48 he started, with very little money in his pocket, to work his passage to New York, designing thence to go to sea in the hope of mending his health. His first halt was at Homer, where he hired himself out as a machinist; and although it was a trade which he had never tried before, the discovery was not made in the shop that he was a raw hand. At Homer he remained, working for seventy-five cents a day, till he had earned enough to carry him to New York, making the journey by canal and steamboat. There he found a sloop in the coasting trade, upon which he shipped to work for his board, and paid his last quarter of a dollar to have his tool chest carried across the city. He remained on board this sloop nearly all summer, and in the autumn, being somewhat improved in health, found his way to Boston, where he engaged for a time in joiner work. But though he was a cunning workman in wood, an idea was brewing in his mind which must find articulation in iron, and he was eager to get into a machine shop. Finding a place in the locomotive works of Hinckley & Drury, he started across the city with his tool chest—all his wealth—when he was suddenly attacked with homesickness. The crooked streets of Boston looked unspeakably hateful to him; he could not bear the thought of tarrying there another day; and as he drew near the Western Railroad depot, he told the expressman with whom he was riding to stop and unload his chest on that platform. The first train carried him as far west as Pittsfield, and that was about as far as his money would go. Here he engaged in cabinet-making and carving, stipulating for his evenings; for the idea which had been buzzing in his brain ever since that winter of 1847–8 must be caught and caged. Wilson says that the machine was invented during that enforced idleness in his own home in Cortland County, and that ill-health alone delayed its construction. Here, at Pittsfield, in the leisure of his evenings, he built the first machine. The dream was a reality. The reality was better than the dream. From the start the machine worked beautifully. It could be improved; but, just as it was, it was a triumph of mechanical genius. Parts of the first machine were made of wood, and Wilson wished to make it all of iron. The facilities for doing machinists' work were not good in Pittsfield; so he carried with him to North Adams the iron parts (which still remain in his possession), and hiring out again as a cabinet maker, employed his leisure in perfecting his invention. Mr. J. N. Chapin, of North Adams, entered into partnership with him in the construction of the machine, and several were built. Meantime trouble was brewing. Elias Howe, Jr., and Isaac M. Singer had produced sewing machines, for which they were endeavoring to obtain patents, and each claimed priority of invention over the other, and over Wilson. Lawsuits were threatened, and Mr. Chapin, an excellent but cautious man, whose honesty and friendship Wilson never doubted, sold out his interest in the patent, and withdrew. While Wilson was in New York, waiting for the issue of the patent, he invented the rotary hook, one of the most exquisite mechanical contrivances ever produced, and otherwise essentially modified his machine. Falling in with Mr. Nathaniel Wheeler, Mr. Wilson entered into partnership with him, and the improved machine took the name of the firm of Wheeler and Wilson.

There has been considerable controversy both in the courts and in the public prints about priority of invention, and the honor has commonly been conferred with some flourish of trumpets upon Mr. Elias Howe, Jr., but these two things are certainly true:

1. Mr. Wilson invented a sewing machine, without help or suggestion from Mr. Howe or anybody else, and without ever having seen or heard of a sewing machine. The idea was purely original with him.

2. The Wheeler and Wilson Machine was a practical success from the beginning, distancing the Howe from the start in the markets of the world. *It was the first practical sewing machine ever made.*

When Mr. Wilson left North Adams for New York with his model in his valise to secure his patent, in the spring of 1850, it is not likely that he, or any of those who knew him, expected that he would return, in the summer of 1865, with the Wilson House in his pocket. This massive pile of brick and iron is only a small part of the earnings of that cunning little workman whose low song has cheered so many tired women. With a kindly feeling toward the town where the sun first began to shine upon him, and where the

WILSON HOUSE, NORTH ADAMS.

best of fortunes came to him in the excellent wife who has been to him a help-meet indeed in his subsequent career, Mr. Wilson resolved to devote a portion of his gains to the erection of this Hotel.

The Wilson House is, as you have already discovered, a first-class hotel. Eight large stores, a fine Public Hall, a Masonic Hall, a Manufacturers' Club Room, and a Billiard Room are included within its walls; and besides its spacious offices, its ample dining-rooms, its large and well appointed kitchens, pantries, store-rooms, its excellent baths, and its elegant parlors, it offers to guests a hundred airy and well-furnished chambers. The Post Office and the Telegraph Office are in the house; the two railroad stations are within three minutes walk; and the stages of the tunnel line leave its doors. Over it preside two genial and attentive landlords, of both of whom, if it were not too much like boasting of its friends, this little book could say a thousand things in praise. However, "good wine needs no bush," and a hotel as good as this needs no strenuous puffing.

WALKS.

After a bath and a breakfast, a walk to the *Natural Bridge* will be in order. Up Main street to Eagle street, then northward past the Eagle Mill and up the hill, turning first to the eastward, then to the northward, then, when the top of the hill is reached, into a cross-road running eastward. The view from this hill top is magnificent. The village, Greylock, the South

Adams valley, and the Williamstown valley, are all in full view. The objects are the same that you saw from the top of the Hoosac Mountain, but you have given the kaleidoscope a turn and the new combination adds a new glory. There is hardly a better view of the Greylock group then you get at this point. Between the main ridge of the mountain and the southern valley there is a lower ridge; the deep gulf that separates the higher mountain from the lower one is called the Notch; and the upper end of the Notch is the Bellows Pipe. Greylock proper, is the highest peak, just west of the Bellows Pipe. Mount Williams is the northern end of this high ridge, which overlooks the village; Mount Fitch is the elevation of the ridge, midway between Greylock and Williams; and the western peak of the mountain, overlooking Williamstown, is Mount Prospect.

The cross-road that we follow eastward from the top of the hill leads us down into the ravine through which flows Hudson's Brook. Under the little wooden bridge the water roars and rushes down the narrow channel it has chiseled for itself in the limestone; below the road is a chasm about fifteen feet wide, from thirty to sixty feet deep and thirty rods long, spanned by an arch of solid rock. Before the days of the white men, the water ran over this rock, and descended in a cascade into the gorge below; but finding some small opening under the rock which is now the Natural Bridge, it has gradually worn this channel to its present depth. In the soft limestone the swift water has done much beautiful and curious carving. Just below the arch a well-worn foot-path will conduct you to a rocky prominence where you get an excellent view of the bridge and the chasm.

You can return by the road that follows the brook down to the lower Clarksburg road, and that will lead you past the Beaver and the Glen Mills, through Union street, back to your starting-point. The Natural Bridge is not more than a mile from the hotel, and is easily reached by carriages.

The *Cascade* in the Notch Brook is a mile and a half from the hotel; and those who dare not venture upon so long a walk can ride up the Williamstown road, past the cemetery to the little drab factory village of Braytonville with its large brick mill, where a road running south past a long red school-house leads up to a saw-mill. Here alighting and fastening your steeds you have less than half a mile to walk. The path follows the Notch Brook through the fields up into a rough and romantic glen, along the sides of which a foot-path leads you till you are stopped by the precipice down which the water is plunging. The perpendicular descent of the water is less than thirty feet, but the walls of the chasm rise much higher. From the very brink of the precipice on either side spring stately forest trees that lock their branches across the abyss, and almost hide the sky. The jagged walls of rock are covered with beautiful growths of ferns and mosses and lichens. Climb to the top of the western cliff, and follow the foot-paths that will lead you to all the best points of view; then lie down in silence upon some mossy bank in sight of the tumbling waters and yield yourself to the spell which the wild grandeur of the scene will work upon you.

Those who have left no steeds behind them will do well to follow the foot-path up the western bank of the ravine, through the woods into the pastures, where they will have a near view of the narrow trough between the mountains known as the Notch. Here they may cross the brook and follow the wood road on the eastern side, that will lead them through the woods and pastures, over the hill and down into the village. It is the road that passes the marble quarries, in full view from the village. The village is supplied with water from the Notch Brook. The dam is half a mile above the cascade, and the road by which we return passes the main reservoir on the top of the hill, and the distributing reservoir upon the eastern slope. The lower reservoir is high enough to give the water tremendous force in the village, furnishing a valuable safeguard against fire. A hose attached to a hydrant will throw a stream through a nozzle an inch and a half in diameter to the height of one hundred and twenty-five feet. Two or three of these streams will drown the fiercest fire in a twinkling; witness the numerous blackened frames about the village too well saved. Not only to these lower uses does this water minister. It feeds the little fountains that sparkle with what Mr. Poe would call "a crystalline delight" along the public ways in the village.

CASCADE IN THE NOTCH BROOK, NORTH ADAMS.

As you descend the hill by this road, the view is charming. The town shows here to good advantage; the Hoosac Range is grandly outlined on the western horizon, and the meadows above the village, through which the winding path of the little river is marked by the willows, are always delightfully fresh and green.

Colegrove's Hill is north of the village. At the head of Eagle street two roads diverge, both running north. Take the right hand road, and at the end of it follow the path through a pasture, in which a clump of tall pines is standing, to the top of a round hill. The view is the same that you had on the walk to the Natural Bridge, but wider and more complete.

Mount Adams invites the pedestrian to climb its easy slope by various paths in view from the village; and promises him an abundant reward for his toil.

Church Hill is at the upper end of Main street. It is quickly reached, and the views which it affords of the gorge through which the north branch flows, and of the South Adams valley, are both excellent.

In short, it may be said that while the streets of the village offer few stylish promenades, all men and women who have stout shoes, short skirts and a love of the beautiful may find, by climbing any hill road or mountain path in the region, a prospect that will delight the eye, an appetite that will make the plainest food delicious, and that unfretted bodily fatigue which brings sweet and refreshing sleep.

DRIVES.

Now, good traveler, we can offer you an entertainment whose variety is almost unbounded and whose delight is perpetual. Perhaps you have heard other New England villages boast of the drives in their neighborhood. Each several town in this Commonwealth, if we may take the testimony of its inhabitants, is approached on every side by country roads of the most remarkable beauty; affording splendid views, and leading through delightful places. Just as all parents believe their children to be the brightest and best of the race, so all New England villagers regard the drives about their several villages as the most beautiful in the world. Eyes that are anointed with love can see beauty in the face of the homeliest child, and discern untold dignity and worth in the dullest human soul; and there is some excellent oil by which the eyes of men in every place are touched to an appreciation of the natural beauty that surrounds them. The added testimony of the villagers is a tribute to the glory of the creation. All these scenes are beautiful. Skies, forests, green meadows, fields of grain, hills and valleys, brooks and lakes and rivers are always beautiful; and they furnish to those who dwell among them, an enjoyment of which they never grow weary.

As for the children, however, you and I, my dear madam, are not surprised that Stubbs and his wife should think for themselves that their baby is beautiful, but surely they cannot expect us to think so. It is natural for every parent to admire his own children; but it would be absurd for some parents to expect other folks to admire their children. However, there are *some* children, ours for instance, whom everybody *must* admire. No one can *help* acknowledging that *they* are the handsomest and most intelligent children anywhere to be found. That is too obvious to be argued about. And in like manner, those of us who live in North Adams, do not wonder that the average New England villager admires, in a general way, the scenery of his neighborhood. It is quite commendable in him to do so. And yet, it would be absurd in him to insist that *we* should go into ecstacies over his frog-ponds and sheep-pastures. But *our* drives, of course, are quite incomparable. Everybody will say that there is nothing like them in Massachusetts. Which, my dear madam, there is not. You have heard of the Berkshire Hills. These upon which you have been looking in your walks, and to which we shall further introduce you in your drives are the Berkshire Hills. And it is safe to say that until you came to North Adams you had never seen any Berkshire Hills worth mentioning, unless, indeed, you had visited Mount Washington, in the south-eastern corner of the county. People sometimes go to Lenox or Stockbridge or Pittsfield, and imagine that they have visited the hills of Berkshire. Now these are all very respectable towns, and quite worth going to see; but the supposition that one finds the Berkshire Hills within their borders is a very good joke indeed. One who has never seen the Deerfield Gorge or the Adams Valley from Hoosac Mountain; who has never climbed to the top of Prospect, or Bald Mountain, or Mount Hopkins, or Greylock; who has never invaded the awful stillness of that sacred place which is known by the profane name of the Hopper,—such a person should talk modestly of Berkshire scenery. He may have seen elsewhere in Berkshire, some very pretty views, and, if Mount Everett and Bashbish have come within the range of his travels, some grand ones,—but with this latter exception, the only scenery in Berkshire that is really notable for grandeur, is in these three towns of Florida, Adams, and Williamstown. It is true that Greylock may be seen on a clear day with the naked eye from Pittsfield and other towns in Southern Berkshire, but one who looks upon it from that distance cannot even conjecture the grand configurations of mountain forms, that are visible here from any valley, or the marvellous magnificence of the prospect from any of these summits. Mountains are to the traveler, what his best achievements are to the wise man, beautiful not so much in themselves as in the outlook they afford. And they who look from the slightly undulating surfaces of Southern Berkshire upon the outline of Greylock in the northern horizon, know but little of the sublimity of the visions they might have if they would climb to his top. Visiting the Berkshire Hills without going north of Pittsfield, is like the play of Hamlet with a good likeness of Hamlet in the upper left hand corner of the drop scene, and no other hint or mention of him during the performance.

Our first drive shall be along a charming valley road to a place of precious memory,—dear and sacred old

WILLIAMSTOWN.

Just beyond Braytonville the highway crosses the Troy and Boston Railroad; the white house and farm buildings of Mr. Bradford Harrison are on the right, and on the left, in the meadow, twenty or thirty rods from the railroad, a small elm tree is growing. That tree was planted by students of Williams College, in the year 1857, to mark the site of old Fort Massachusetts.

During the French and Indian wars, the invading forces from Canada more frequently followed the course of the Connecticut River southward into Massachusetts; but occasionally they came down by way of Lake Champlain, the Hudson and the Hoosac Valleys, crossing the Hoosac Mountain at this point, and following the Deerfield River down to the Connecticut. To protect the settlements against these incursions Fort Massachusetts was built, about 1744. It does not require any profound knowledge of military science to discover that the fort was badly placed. The rocky bluffs on the north were within rifle range, and from them an enemy could look down into the stockade and ascertain the strength of its garrison. "A judicious choice of posts," says General Hoyt, "and the principles of fortifications, though probably understood by the *engineers* of the time, seem not to have been regarded in early wars. Most of these works were built on low grounds, often in the vicinity of commanding heights, generally constructed of single stockades without ditches or flanking posts, capable only of a direct fire, and against the lightest artillery untenable." But what these pioneer soldiers lacked in science they made up in courage. Fort Massachusetts is poorly located, but it was defended by some of the bravest men that ever lived; and it was the scene of one of the pluckiest fights recorded in our history.

Captain (afterward Colonel) Ephraim Williams was the first commander of the defences in this neighborhood, and his head-quarters were in Fort Massachusetts. During the summer of 1746 an expedition against Canada was projected, Captain Williams was summoned to Albany to join it, and the garrison was left in the charge of Sergeant John Hawks with only twenty-two effective men. After the departure of Captain Williams, Indians were seen prowling about the heights, north of the fort; and on the 20th of August, a force of nine hundred French and Indians, under the command of General Rigaud de Vandreuil, seized this hill on the right of the road where the chestnut woods now stand, and sent to Sergeant Hawks a demand for the surrender of the fort. The sergeant had no artillery, and but a poor supply of ammunition; but he promptly rejected the proposal of the French commander, and with his twenty-two brave men defended the fort for twenty-eight hours against the overwhelming force of the enemy. Every Indian or Frenchman who came out from the safe cover of the forest was a target for these twenty-two sharp-shooters; and some were killed at the long range of sixty rods. The ammunition of the garrison was finally exhausted, and Hawks capitulated, making the condition that his forces should be humanely treated as prisoners of war, and should not be delivered to the Indians. The French commander accepted his terms of capitulation, and perfidiously violated them the following day by surrendering half of the prisoners into the hands of the Indians. One man who was sick and unable to march was killed by the savages; the others were taken to Canada as prisoners, and were finally exchanged. The assailants lost forty-seven men before the fort; while of the brave little garrison only one was killed. The bravery of Sergeant Hawks was rewarded by promotion; afterward, in the war of 1755 he rose to the rank of lieutenant-colonel. "Bold, hardy and enterprising, he acquired the confidence and esteem of his superior officers and was entrusted with important commands. He was no less valued by the inhabitants of Deerfield, his native town, for his civil qualities."*

The ambuscade at the *Bars* in the Deerfield Meadow, to which allusion has already been made, was formed by a party of these Indians under Vandreuil, who crossed the mountain after the surrender of the fort and made their way to Deerfield. The fort was demolished by its captors, but was rebuilt and more strongly garri-

* Hoyt's Indian Wars, p. 238.

soned during the following year. In all the subsequent wars with the French and Indians, until the Peace of Paris in 1763 this fort was a post of much importance, and frequent mention is made of it in the old histories.

From the time of the building of the fort until 1755, the command of the forces and the defences of this region devolved as we have seen, upon Colonel Ephraim Williams, a native of Newton, and one of the first settlers of Stockbridge. Though frequently called to active service elsewhere his head-quarters were at this fort, and with the few settlers who occupied this valley he had thoroughly identified himself, sharing their perils and privations, and studying their welfare. In the year 1735, Colonel Williams, then in command of a regiment, was summoned to join General Johnson, whose head-quarters were then at the head of Lake George, near the site of the present village of Caldwell. On his way to this post, with an apparent presentiment of his fate, the Colonel halted at Albany and made his will on the 22d of July; in which, after several bequests to his relatives and friends he directed "that the remainder of his land should be sold at the discretion of his executors within five years after an established peace; and that the interest of the monies arising from the sale, and also the interest of his notes and bonds, should be applied to the support of a free school in a township west of Fort Massachusetts, forever; provided said township fall within Massachusetts, on running the line between Massachusetts and New

York; and providing the said township when incorporated shall be called Williamstown."

On the 8th of September, following, he was despatched from the camp on Lake George at the head of twelve hundred men upon a most important and hazardous enterprise; and falling into an ambuscade of French and Indians was shot through the head. His body was buried near the spot where he fell, on the right of the road running from Glen's Falls to Caldwell, and in the vicinity of Bloody Pond, a lakelet which on that day received its terrible christening. A large rock has always been pointed out as marking the spot where he fell; and upon this rock the students of Williams College a few years ago erected a marble monument, with an appropriate inscription. The writer of this book well remembers descending one midnight from the stage-coach in which, a lonely passenger, he was making his way over the old war-path from Lake George to the Hudson; and clambering under the light of the stars up the rude foot-path to the rock among the bushes, where the little marble obelisk guards the dust of this brave and good soldier.

The provision in the will of Colonel Williams was the foundation of Williams College. The sum thus bequeathed was increased by donations of individuals, and by a pious lottery which the Legislature granted to the trustees of the fund, until, in 1790, the solid walls of old West College were erected, and a considerable fund was placed at interest to assist in maintaining the school. It consisted at first of two depart-

ments—an academy or grammar school and an English free school, and was under the care of Mr. Ebenezer Fitch, a graduate of Yale. In 1793 it was erected into a college, and the first class, numbering four, was graduated September 2, 1795. Dr. Fitch continued at the head of the college till 1815, and was succeeded by Rev. Zephaniah Swift Moore, D. D. An effort was made in 1818 to transfer the college to Northampton, but after a stormy and protracted contest the Legislature decided against a change of location. Upon this, Dr. Moore who had favored the removal, resigned the presidency; and Rev. Edward Dorr Griffin, of great fame as a theologian and a pulpit orator, was called to succeed him. Under his administration the college which had been in a low condition for several years, regained its prosperity. In 1836, he was compelled by declining health to withdraw from the position which he had so abundantly honored, and his mantle fell upon one who was worthy to wear it, and who for thirty-three years has worn it worthily. Wonderful aptitude for teaching, great prudence and skill in administration, dignity of demeanor and purity of character have made him the most revered and most illustrious, as he is now the oldest college president in the land; while his contributions to philosophy and his active participation in the various enterprises of Christian benevolence, have gained for him the admiration and confidence of good men everywhere. Under the management of President Hopkins and his efficient coadjutors in the faculty, the college has advanced to a

leading position. The number of students is not so large as in some of our New England colleges, varying from two hundred to two hundred and fifty, but the instruction is all given by professors of experience, instead of being entrusted, as in many colleges, to incompetent tutors; thus securing a thoroughness not easily attainable under the other system.

From this valley road the profile of the mountain on the south resembles a saddle; and this likeness gave to this group of hills of which Greylock is the central eminence, the ugly name of Saddle Mountain, by which it is known in the geographies. The highest of the two peaks visible at this point, and the one nearest North Adams, is Mount Williams; the other is Mount Prospect.

Just beyond Fort Massachusetts, in the center of the valley, is the Greylock Cotton Mill, amid its cluster of drab cottages.

Blackinton is the name of the neat white factory village a mile further west. The woolen mill of S. Blackinton & Son built the village and one of the largest fortunes in Berkshire. The little brown wooden building in which the senior proprietor begun the business, working with his own hands,—is standing a little west of the mill. We cross the railroad and the river by a covered bridge beyond Blackinton, and soon after ascend a little eminence in the road from which the whole valley opens magnificently. In the west, and running far to the north are the Taghkanic Hills with their swelling slopes and their wavy outlines;

between them and the hill on our right, which is a continuation of Mount Adams, and is known on this side indifferently as Oak Hill and East Mountain, the green valley of the Hoosac narrows to a gorge in the north-west; in the northern horizon The Dome, a noble and symmetrical peak, is built up into the sky; on the south the wooded ridge of Prospect stretches away toward the Hopper, the opening of which is scarcely visible; in the east beyond the narrow opening between Mount Adams and the southern group the massive battlements of the Hoosac Mountain close the scene. Within this circle of hills a most charming valley is included. Observe the beautiful variety of surface; the natural grouping of the trees upon the slopes; the picturesque and park-like appearance of the whole landscape.

Soon we pass through the factory grounds at the lower end of the village; cross another covered bridge, ascend a little hill and find ourselves at the foot of the broad and shady street on which the old village is built. Williamstown, like Boston, boasts its three hills, each of which in its day was crowned with historic edifices, but from one of them the glory has departed. At the top of the first hill on the right stands Griffin Hall,—once the chapel, but now containing the college cabinet, and the head-quarters of the Natural History Department. In front of Griffin Hall upon the brow of the hill is the soldiers' monument—a freestone shaft, surmounted by the bronze statue of a soldier,—erected in honor of the Williams boys who fell in the late war.

Just beyond Griffin Hall is Goodrich Hall, a noble stone edifice, the gift of Hon. John Z. Goodrich of Stockbridge, containing the Gymnasium, the Bowling Alley, and the Chemical Laboratory. Across the street are East and South Colleges,—dormitories occupied by the Senior and Junior Classes. Lawrence Hall is an octagonal building named in honor of Amos Lawrence, one of the most liberal patrons of the college; which contains the Library, the collection of portraits of graduates, and some sculptures in bas-relief from ancient Nineveh. Just beyond Lawrence Hall is the Chapel with Alumni Hall in the rear. Southeast of the group of buildings, nearly hidden from the street by the foliage, is the Astronomical Observatory—the first one built on this continent—the Magnetic Observatory, and Jackson Hall, built by Nathan Jackson, Esq., of New York, another generous friend of the college, and occupied by the Lyceum of Natural History. The tower of this building commands an excellent view of the valley and its encircling hills. The new Congregational Church is on the right beyond this first group of college buildings. On the top of the next hill, old West College, the original Academy and Free School, erected in 1790, stands on the left. This building and Kellogg Hall in its rear, are dormitories for the Sophomore and Freshman Classes. The President's mansion is opposite West College.

At the head of the street, upon the western eminence, perished by fire, three winters ago, the old Congregational Meeting-House. Williamstown street without the old church at the head of it, is a song without a cadence. To many of the graduates, Williamstown will never be quite herself again, now that the old church is no more.

Just beyond West College we turn to the right into a street leading to Mills Park, an enclosure of ten acres, in which a marble shaft surmounted by a globe, marks the spot where Samuel J. Mills and his associates met by a hay-stack in 1807, to consecrate themselves to the work of foreign missions. That was the beginning in America of this great enterprise of Christian benevolence.

Returning to the principal street, we go on westward and turn to the north at the Mansion House. Following the road through the valley at the foot of the Taghkanic range for a mile and a half, we turn to the right into a cross-road which leads up to a little group of plain brown buildings with a sloping green in front of them. These are the little hostelry and bathing-houses of the Williamstown Mineral Spring,—known to fame in these quarters, and among graduates of Williams College everywhere, as the "Sand Spring." The temperature of the water, the supply of which is abundant, is about 70° Fahrenheit the year round; and while it is said to be a valuable alterative and tonic in many diseases, it furnishes one of the most delicious baths ever enjoyed by mortals. In the cure of cutaneous diseases these baths are said to be remarkably efficacious. How true this may be with regard to other forms of skin disease we know not; but for that form of the disease which is most prevalent and most fatal,—known among the ancients as *spurcitia* or ακαϑαρϛία, and among the moderns by a name so common that it is hardly worth while to repeat it, they are certainly a specific. In the little bathing-house you will find swimming baths, plunge baths, shower baths, and all necessary conveniences for the refreshment and purification of the outer man. Give them a thorough trial and you will return to you lodgings cleaner, handsomer, happier and better men and women.

SOUTH ADAMS AND THE NOTCH.

The East Road to South Adams is the continuation of South Church street. For the first two miles it runs between the mountain and a series of diluvial hillocks that stand at its base. These conical mounds frequently occur in the country, but they are not often found so symmetrically disposed as at this point. They are composed of sand and gravel, and so regular are they in form that it is easy to suppose them to be the work of human hands. The earlier theory was that they were erected by the primitive races, either as fortifications or as burial mounds; and this theory has found poetical expression in one of Whittier's latest and best lyrics,—"The Grave by the Lake." But the geologists say, (and who can confute the geologists?) that these mounds were caused by the action of water; though just how the water could have piled them up in their present forms they do not tell us very definitely.

Two miles south of the village a mound is seen on the left hand side of the road which, it is pretty safe to conjecture, is the work of men's hands. It is composed of the earth taken out of the open cutting at the western portal of the Hoosac Tunnel. The embankment of the railroad is built as far as the highway, and the road to the tunnel follows the embankment. For an account of what is to be seen at this point the reader is referred to the preceding chapter.

Having "done" the west end and the west shaft in much less time than the Messrs. Shanly with all their energy will require to do them; and having explored, if we have a taste for such explorations, the Nitro-glycerine Works near the shaft where Mr. Mowbray manufactures the mild mixture, whose liquid eloquence so gently persuades the rocks asunder, we go on southward. Two miles beyond the tunnel we reach an eminence in the road upon which we shall do well to pause and look about us. At the head of the valley in the north, walled in on three sides by the mountains, lies the village of North Adams; before us is South Adams, and the beautiful hills beyond, in Cheshire, and Savoy; between these two villages the eye ranges over the whole six miles of fertile valley—a carpet of cunning patterns and matchless coloring, seamed by the railway and embroidered by the river; and directly opposite, across the valley is the majestic front of Greylock, rising abruptly from the plain below to a height of three thousand feet above the river bed and thirty-five hundred feet above tide water.

HOOSAC TUNNEL—WESTERN PORTAL.

A mile further on the road follows a brook down into the village of South Adams through which we may drive briskly; admiring the enterprise that keeps so many mills running busily, the public spirit that has built so fine a school-house as the one we see upon the hill, and the taste that has begun as in North Adams to ornament and improve the private residences and grounds.

Near the depot a street leads westward directly toward the base of Greylock; that we follow to the old Quaker Meeting-House, then turn to the right into the mountain road that leads over the lower ridge of the Greylock group into the Notch. There is hard climbing before us, but we shall have our reward. As soon as we reach that eminence just above us, we will look backward. On our right the Hoosac range lifts up its level rampart—southward the lines of the horizon are broken by the bolder peaks of the Cheshire mountains. Just below us, in the widening of the valley lies South Adams, and beyond it are the eastward slopes, over which the Williamsburg and North Adams Railroad is to run through Savoy. It is a very pretty picture, but we must not stay to look upon it, for there are richer prospects before us. A little further on we flank a forest that has stood between us and the valley on our right, and reach a point from which we can look right down into the beautiful meadows through which the Hoosac River runs. Did grass ever grow greener than the grass of those meadows, or was sunshine ever brighter than this golden flood that fills the valley with its splendor? Look at the river with its willow fringes winding down through the meadows. Plainly it is in no hurry. In its quiet search of coolness and beauty it explores the whole valley. More than once it goes back as if it had forgotten something,—to bathe some thirsty cresses perhaps, or to sing its low sweet song in the shade of some alder-bushes. The river had a hard passage through South Adams. It had to go through the mill—several mills, indeed. The water-wheels churned it into foam; the flumes led it through dark and perilous passages; the dyers stained its purity with logwood and copperas. It was made a menial servant and a scavenger. It did not enjoy town life, at all. And now that it has escaped into the quiet country again, it means to make the most of the country delights. So it lingers as long as it can in these green fields, and among these sedges. If it only knew what it must pass through at North Adams it would stay even longer, I think.

While we have been looking down into this valley, our steed has been tugging up a steep acclivity, and suddenly, as we reach the top, there opens before us a new scene. I think we can afford now to let our horse have a breathing spell. A panorama opens before us here, that we shall not tire of looking at till he is rested. Far away to the northward opens the valley through which the north branch of the Hoosac flows down from the mountains of Vermont. On the east the Hoosac range stretches away toward the north as far as the eye can see: from the hills of Savoy behind us to the northern horizon in Readsboro, there must be nearly twenty miles of this straight unbroken mountain chain, whose eastern slope is in full view. On the east our vision is bounded by the range of which Mount Adams is the southern abutment. Between these two ranges the valley stretches away narrowing toward its northern extremity till it is lost in the blue distance between the hills. This view is not so extensive as the view from Greylock or Mount Hopkins or the farther side of the Hoosac Mountain, but one would hardly be willing to admit that it is less beautiful than the fairest of them.

Going on a little farther we reach a little eminence, from which the view is widened somewhat; the northern portion of North Adams comes into plain view, and Mount Adams confronts us with its solid grandeur of outline.

Now we turn to the westward, passing on the left the signal station built by Mr. Doane for keeping the range of the tunnel,—and begin a rapid descent. To timid persons this may seem a perilous passage, but the road is smooth, and with a skillful driver, a steady horse and a stout harness there is not a particle of danger. If you were inclined to be afraid the laughing of this little brook by the roadside would reassure you. Soon we emerge from the thicket of low birches and wild cherry trees through which we have been winding and find ourselves in the Notch. On the one side rises the steep flank of the mountain over which we have just passed—on the other tower Greylock, Fitch and Williams—a trinity of majestic mountain peaks. Now you see the reason why the wind blows so furiously here in winter. The north-west gales coming up the Hoosac Valley are stopped in their course by the northern spur of the hill over which we have passed; and instead of following the river to South Adams they take this shorter course through the Notch. At its southern end the Notch grows narrow and if you stand at the very extremity of it, where it opens into the south Adams Valley on some windy day in March, you would be able to understand why it has been called the Bellows Pipe. It may occur to some travelers that no name has been given to the ridge over which we have just climbed,—which runs parallel with the Greylock ridge and extends from the marble quarries at North Adams nearly to the village of South Adams. Until now it has been nameless, as it certainly does not deserve to be. A mountain that affords so grand a prospect, and the highest peak of which rises not less than two thousand five hundred feet above the level of the sea—nearly three times as high as the famous Mount Holyoke might claim at least the barren honor of a name. By what name shall it be called? That gallant soldier whose heroism is recorded in this chapter,—who held what Mr. Everett called the Thermopylæ of New England, so bravely for so many hours, against such fearful odds, is without honor in the country he defended by his valor. The soldier deserves a monument; the mountain deserves a name; why may we not fittingly write the soldier's name upon the mountain, and let MOUNT

HAWKS perpetuate the memory of a man whom Massachusetts cannot afford to forget.

When we emerge from the Notch, we follow the road around the base of Mount Williams to a point on the western slope of the hill, where we turn sharply to the right and descend. If, however, we are not too weary, we shall find it to our account to drive westward for a mile or more along the road that follows the top of the bluff. Near the foot of Prospect, we may halt upon the top of a declivity where the best view is obtained of the Taghkanic range. The bold outline of these beautiful hills, the deep ravines that furrow their sides, and the transverse ridges that are built like buttresses against their solid wall, are grandly shown at this point. From any point of this bluff, as well as from the road by which we descend when we return, the view of the Hoosac Valley, overlooked by the beautiful Williamstown upon its classic heights, holding in its lap the busy Blackinton and Greylock, and parted by the winding river that turns with equal facility the wheels of the mills and the sentences of the sophomores, is a view not to be missed by any sojourner among the hills of Berkshire.

MOUNT HOPKINS

is the highest peak of the Taghkanic chain. As you pass over the hill at the Cemetery, going toward Williamstown, it lies directly before you. One of the indentations in the horizon is cleared of timber for some distance; on the right of this clearing are two bold peaks that are nameless; on the left is Mount Hopkins. Its twin summits, with but little distance or depression between them, bear the name of the honored President of Williams College and his no less honored brother, Professor Albert Hopkins, who for many years has occupied the chair of Natural Philosophy and Astronomy in Williams College; whose enterprise built the Astronomical and the Magnetic Observatories; whose taste adorned the College grounds; whose name is the synonym of the truest Christian integrity, and whose love of nature has qualified him to be her chief interpreter in all this region. No man knows the beauty of Berkshire so well, no man loves it with so pure an enthusiasm as Professor Hopkins. The tribute of respect which is paid to him in bestowing his name upon this mountain is but a slight recognition of what he has done to lead his neighbors and his pupils into the knowledge and the love of the true, the good and the beautiful.

The road to Mount Hopkins leads through Williamstown; turns to the left, just beyond the site of the old church; a mile further on, descends to the left, at another parting of the ways, into a deep ravine; at the end of another mile, turns to the right through a beautiful wood; after emerging from which, it passes an old school-house, and keeps to the left up a hill, the top of which is reached by difficult climbing, when we find ourselves in the clearing upon which we looked from the Cemetery hill. At this point, the eastern view of Greylock, the Hopper on its western side, the Adams

Valley, the Hoosac Mountains beyond, and the western view of the deep valleys and the billowy hills stretching away for thirty miles toward the valley of the Hudson, are to a lowlander somewhat notable. Turning to the left, into the pasture, we follow a wagon track up a steep acclivity, and pass through a wood into a clearing. An old cellar marks the site of a farm-house which once stood here. What could have induced any human being to build for himself a habitation upon this mountain top it is difficult to guess. We pass through another wood, and emerge at length into a clearing upon the summit of Mount Hopkins, from which the view is perfect in every direction. On the north are the Green Mountains of Vermont; on the east Greylock, whose grandeur you never have known till you have looked upon him from this summit; on the south the Taghkanic range and the valleys that divide it, and on the west the magnificent reach of cultivated hills. The boats on the Hudson can be seen with a glass on a clear day. The view on the south is perhaps the longest remembered. Here as hardly anywhere else in this region one gets an impression of the stupendous forces that have reared these mountain ridges.

This summit is two thousand eight hundred feet above tide-water, and it is reached in a carriage, without great difficulty, by a two hours' ride from North Adams. The tourist should be provided with a compass, a field-glass, a lunch and warm wrappings; he should get an early start that he may enjoy the western view with the sun at his back, and he should drive homeward at the close of the afternoon.

Of the other excursions that may be made from North Adams the mention must be brief. Among those more distant we may mention the drive to *Mount Anthony* near Bennington, where from an observatory one hundred and fifty feet high an extended and diversified view is obtained of the whole of this mountainous region.

The excursion to *Pittsfield,* through Williamstown and Lanesboro, passing Pontoosuc Lake, is easy and delightful. To make it perfect, cross the Taghkanic range from Pittsfield to New Lebanon, visit the SHAKERS, spend the night at the Springs, and return the next day through Hancock and South Williamstown.

Snow Glen is a deep fissure on the western side of the Taghkanics, beyond Williamstown, where snow may be found in midsummer. The western prospect is similar to that from Mount Hopkins, but less beautiful. The carriage road passes within two miles of the glen, and the rest of the journey must be made on foot.

Among the drives in the immediate vicinity of North Adams, one of the most beautiful follows the north branch of the Hoosac to *Stamford;* returning leaves the valley road at a crossing near a school-house, and follows the base of the Hoosac Mountain, passing one road that turns to the right, and after that keeping to the right till it reaches the "*Five Points*" a mile east of the village of North Adams.

The view from the farm-house of Mr. Joseph Wheeler,

whose red buildings are seen from the village on the side of Mount Adams is a delightful one. In short it may be said of the drives as of the walks, that there is no road leading out of North Adams from which you may not gain, without traveling far, prospects which, to use the Frenchman's climax, are either magnificent, sublime, or pretty good.

TO THE TOP OF GREYLOCK.

We have been under the shadow of Greylock long enough to have some desire to climb to his summit. To have had this view first would have dulled our enjoyment of the scenes upon which we have been looking. Moreover, this tramp to the top of Greylock requires some physical stamina, and it is fair to suppose that those who have spent a week in the bracing air of these Berkshire Hills are in better condition for such an undertaking than they were when they came. There was good reason, therefore, for keeping the good wine till the end of the feast.

At the time of the writing of these pages it is difficult to give full information as to the best way of ascending Greylock. Three different roads have been followed, all of which have their advantages. One climbs Bald Mountain, south of the Hopper; another ascends the southern side of the mountain from South Adams; the third leaves the Notch Road at the house of Mr. Walden, winds round the northern end of Mount Williams, passes through a clearing known as Wilbur's Pasture between Williams and Prospect; then climbs the ridge on its western side, and follows it southward to the clearing on the top of Greylock. At present these roads are all bad; a long tramp must be taken after carriages and horses are left behind; but movements are now on foot to improve one or more of them, so that it may be possible to reach the top on horseback if not in carriages. The view from the summit is not so good as it would be if a tower were erected there. The top of the mountain is cleared, but the forest that surrounds the clearing, while it does not greatly interfere with the distant view, shuts out from our vision the valleys in the immediate neighborhood, and without a sight of these the prospect is incomplete. A structure of some sort, forty or fifty feet in height, would give us both the near and the distant landscape. Several years ago such a tower was erected, but through accident or mischievous design it was destroyed by fire. It is hoped that another may be erected early in the present season.

Of the roads to the top of Greylock, the one which ascends from South Adams is said to be the easiest; but for grandeur of scenery either of the others is to be preferred. No tourist should fail to visit the Hopper whether he ascends the mountain by that route or not. Following up Money Brook from the South Williamstown road you find yourselves at the entrance of this stupendous amphitheatre of hills. The gorge by which the brook flows out, between Prospect on the north and Bald Mountain on the south is very narrow; and these two mountains, together with Greylock which rises directly before us as we enter, constitute the three sides of this wonderful gulf. Ascending this brook for a mile and a half you may find upon its southern branch the most remarkable waterfall in this region. The water comes down from a great height in successive leaps; the rocks over which it tumbles rise one above another in semicircular tiers like the seats in a theater; and their sides are always green with the most beautiful hanging moss. This is a cascade which has been visited by very few persons, and the writer of this book is not one of them. You have this account, therefore, at second hand, but it is none the less reliable on that account.

It will not do, however, to attempt the exploration of Money Brook and its cascade on the same day in which we climb Greylock. That must be a separate excursion. It is enough before you climb Bald Mountain if you ascend the stream for a little way, that you may gain some adequate impression of the loftiness and steepness of the close mountain walls that form the sides of this enormous gulf.

Ascending now to the top of Bald Mountain, follow its naked summit nearly to its most northerly point, and there the gulf opens before you,—a yawning abyss from which people with nerves are apt to shrink. The chasm is more than a thousand feet in depth, and from the point where you are standing the four sides seem to converge to a point at the bottom. With the exception of a few land-slides this gulf is wooded on all sides from base to summit. The wonder is that these slides are not more frequent, and that the mountains are not denuded of their forests, so precipitous are their sides. Occasional patches of black spruce relieve the lighter foliage of the slopes. Probably this world does not contain a more gorgeous show of autumnal coloring than is visible here in early October.

Passing on from Bald Mountain north-westerly we reach at length the summit of Greylock, and stand upon the highest land in Massachusetts. An enthusiastic person can hardly be trusted to tell what is visible from this summit. "I know of no place," says President Hitchcock, "where the mind is so forcibly impressed by the idea of vastness and even of immensity, as when the eye ranges abroad from this eminence!" Immensity! no smaller word will fit the scene.

The physical geography of the surrounding region is such as to give to this view all the elements of sublimity. A single mountain peak or range, in the midst of a comparatively level country, may afford a prospect of extent, variety and beauty; but it cannot show us the glories that Greylock reveals from his summit. Here is a belt of mountains extending from the Connecticut River nearly to the Hudson—a distance of fifty or sixty miles—and from the sources of the Connecticut River to Long Island Sound. "To regard these highlands," says Dr. Palfrey, "as simply ranges of hills would not be to conceive of them aright. They are vast swells of land of an average elevation of a thousand feet above the level of the sea, . . . from which, as from a base, mountains rise in chains or in isolated groups to an altitude of several thousand feet more." The two mountain ranges which pass through these highlands—the Hoosac and the Taghkanic chains—have, according to the same authority, "a regular increase from south to north. From a height of less than a thousand feet in Connecticut, they rise to an average of twenty-five hundred feet in Massachusetts, where the majestic Greylock, isolated between the two chains, lifts its head to the stature of thirty-five hundred feet." It will be seen, therefore, that Greylock commands a view of exceptional grandeur. Down at his feet lies the valley of the Hoosac, nearly three thousand feet below; Pittsfield, with its beautiful lakes, and many smaller villages, are seen in the valleys and on the adjacent slopes; south-westward the eye sweeps over the top of the Taghkanics, away to the Catskills beyond the Hudson; north-westward the peaks of the Adirondacks, in Northern New York, are plainly visible; in the north the sturdy ridges of the Green Mountains file away in grand outline; on the east Monadnock and Wachusett renew their stately greeting, and Tom and Holyoke look up from their beautiful valley; southward Mount Everett stands sentinel at the portal of Berkshire, through which the Housatonic flows; and all this grand circuit is filled with mountains. Range beyond range, peak above peak, they stretch away on every side, a boundless expanse of mountain summits. Standing here, and taking in with your eye all that is contained within the vague boundaries of the horizon, you receive one of the grandest if not the very first impression you ever had of distance, of immensity, and of illimitable force. It is well if one can see the sunset and the sunrise from this eminence. With a bed of hemlock boughs for a couch and an army blanket for a covering, any robust person of either sex will sleep soundly after the fatigue of the ascent, and a cloudless evening and morning will make amends for any amount of discomfort.

It will be better to return by a different route from that by which we ascended. The road which follows the ridge northward, then descends to the west into Wilbur's Pasture, and winds round Mount Williams to the east, will give us the best outlook. The view from Prospect, the top of which is easily reached from Wilbur's Pasture, is one that we must not miss. Let us hear President Hitchcock:

"On turning northerly, and proceeding to the extremity of the open ground, we come to the steep margin of the mountain, and in a moment the beautiful valley and village of Williamstown burst like a bright vision upon the eye. . . . . I have rarely if ever experienced such a pleasing change from the emotion of beauty to that of sublimity as at this spot. The moment one fixes his eye upon the valley of Williamstown, he cannot but exclaim, 'How beautiful!' But ere he is aware of it, his eye is following up and onward the vast mountain slopes above described, and on the far off horizon he witnesses intervening ridge after ridge peering above one another, until they are lost in the distance, and unconsciously he finds his heart swelling with the emotion of sublimity."

Whether the route we have chosen for the ascent and descent of Greylock will be the one selected for improvement cannot now be stated; but it certainly affords more varied and satisfactory views of the scenery of the Greylock group than any other. If the roads were tolerably good, the tour of the mountain might easily be made in a day; and in the views from the bottom of the Hopper, from the top of Bald Mountain, from the summit of Greylock and from Prospect there would be glory enough for one day.

DOWN THE HOOSAC TO THE HUDSON.

Away from this pleasant valley some faces must turn at last. The shadow of Greylock that has fallen like a benediction upon the weary, must be forsaken for the shorter and hotter shadows of brown-stone walls; and the walks and drives that led to so many mountains of beatitude must be exchanged for the level weariness of city pavements. From the Troy and Boston railroad station you trundle slowly out through the little tunnel, and soon the broad slopes of Mount Adams and the beautiful curves of Williams and Prospect are left behind as you follow the beautiful river down toward the sea. The river and the railroad pass through a corner of Vermont; the two or three villages named Pownal through which you pass, are in that sturdy little State. The two or three Hoosacs which follow are in the State of New York; the larger of these villages being known as Hoosac Falls and distinguished chiefly in these days as the place where the Walter A. Wood Mowing Machine Company has its extensive machine shops. The battle of Bennington was in this town of Hoosac, and the heights upon which it was fought are in view from the railroad just beyond Hoosac Junction. Hoosac Falls is the only important town between North Adams and Troy. The region through which the road runs is a most delightful one, however; much of it fertile and highly cultivated. The Taghkanic Mountains on the one side and the Green Mountains on the other, draw close to the river as we pass through Vermont, but beyond Hoosac the Green Mountains retreat to the north and you look away to the right across a beautiful open country. Still the river windeth at its own sweet will through the meadows, and still you follow it, glad of its pleasant company. Its volume is swollen since you knew it first among the alders in the Adams valley; but unlike some whose fortunes grow, its added floods have robbed it of neither gentleness nor grace.

"Sing soft, sing low, our lowland river,
Under thy banks of laurel bloom;
Softly and sweet as the hour beseemeth,
Sing us the songs of peace and home.

"The cradle-song of thy hill-side fountains
Here in thy glory and strength repeat;
Give us a taste of thy upland music,
Show us the dance of thy silver feet.

"Into thy dutiful life of uses
Pour the music and weave the flowers;
With the song of birds and bloom of meadows,
Lighten and gladden thy heart and hours.

"Sing on! bring down, O lowland river,
The joy of the hills to the waiting sea;
The wealth of the vales, the pomp of mountains,
The breath of the woodlands bear with thee."

But the railroad that was glad to woo the river when the way was hard among the hills, has found that the world is wider, and coolly withdraws to the southward. From the heights along which it leads you, the valley of the Hudson soon appears broad and bright with verdure; from the rocky bluff beyond the valley, the waters of the Mohawk tumble down the cataract that turns the mill-wheels of Cohoes; the twin villages of Waterford and Lansingburgh greet you from their lowly seat by the Hudson; there are street lamps, pavements, flagmen at the crossings; the speed slackens; a vast and smoky roof, with massive iron trusses, hides the sky, and your journey ends where the journey of Æneas begun—within the walls of Troy.

www.ingramcontent.com/pod-product-compliance
Lightning Source LLC
LaVergne TN
LVHW021358110826
845150LV00007B/1694

* 9 7 8 1 4 2 5 5 1 3 1 5 3 *